GW00360129

soho
theatre + writers' centre

Soho Theatre Company presents

SCHOOL PLAY

by **Suzy Almond**

First performed at Soho Theatre and Writers' Centre, 21 Dean Street,
London W1, on 20 June 2001.

LONDON ARTS   SUPPORTED BY CITY OF WESTMINSTER   stone TBWA\GGT DIRECT

Soho Theatre is supported by Stone, Bloomberg and TBWA\GGT Direct.
Performances in the Lorenz Auditorium.
Registered. Charity No: 267234

SCHOOL PLAY

by **Suzy Almond**

Paul	Bryan Dick
Charlie	Brooke Kinsella
Lee	Daniel Scott-Croxford
Miss Fry	Tracy-Ann Oberman

There is no interval.

Director	Jonathan Lloyd
Designer	Luke Hunt
Lighting Designer	Jonathan Rouse
Sound Designer	Nick Blount
Composer	Chris Hoban

Production Manager	Nick Ferguson
Stage Manager	Christine Hathway
Deputy Stage Manager	Anna Graf
Work Placement	Emily Elson/Caroline Beale
Set built and painted by	Robert Knight
Props built and painted by	Fahmida Bakht/Charlotte Gainey
Prop Buyer	Hannah Bentley
Costume Supervisor	James Button
Production Electrician	Seb Baraclough

Soho Theatre Company would like to thank:

The Grey Coat Hospital, Motorola, The Motorcycle Engineering Department at Merton College, Bryan Raven at White Light and Dave Ishwood at the Moving Light Company, Swatch UK, The Firework Company, CRISP, Andrew Tait and the pupils of Bede 9 at St Augustines Primary School, Ellen at The Hollister Independence Rally, Alison Kriel and all at Betty Laywood School, Autograph Sound Studio, Jo Perry, Jo Woods and the terrific pupils in the orchestra class at Quintin Kynaston School: Alex (trombone), Alex Okore (trombone), Stephanie Grieve (trumpet), Mohamed (trumpet), Filloreta Gula (trumpet), Polina Norina (flute), Begaim Tulegenova (violin), Jesse Rutherford (clarinet) and Shaima Al-Obaidi (French horn).

Press Representation Angela Dias at Soho Theatre (020 7478 0142)
Advertising Haymarket Advertising for Guy Chapman Associates
Graphic Design Jane Harper
Publicity Photographs Stuart Colwill

soho
theatre + writers' centre

Soho Theatre and Writers' Centre, 21 Dean Street, London W1D 3NE
Admin: 020 7287 5060 Fax: 020 7287 5061 Box Office: 020 7478 0100
www.sohotheatre.com   email: mail@sohotheatre.com

THE COMPANY

Cast

Bryan Dick, *Paul*

Trained at Lamda. Television includes: *Clocking Off 2*, *North Square*, *The Life and Times of Henry Pratt*, *Bonjour La Classe* and *The Bill*.

Brooke Kinsella, *Charlie*

Trained at Anna Scher Theatre. Television includes: *The Bill*, *Sunburn*, *The Vice*, *Kid in the Corner* and *No Child of Mine* (winner of Best Drama at the BAFTAs).

Tracy-Ann Oberman, *Miss Fry*

Trained at Central School of Speech and Drama. Theatre includes: *Loot* (Vaudeville and Chichester); *Saturday, Sunday and Monday*; *Two* (Chichester); *A Call in the Night* (West Yorkshire Playhouse); *Love for Love* (New End) and *Caught in the Act* (Watford/Chichester). Many RSC productions including: *The Changeling*; *Tamburlaine*; *The Beggars Opera*; *Two Faced* and *Macbeth*. Television includes: *Bob Martin* (Granada TV); *Casualty*; *Happiness*; *Rhona*; *The Way It Is; Marion + Geoff* (BBC) and *Kiss Me Kate* (Carlton). Extensive radio work in both drama and light entertainment. Film: *Killing Time*.

Daniel Scott-Croxford, *Lee*

Trained at Anna Scher Theatre. Television includes: *Eastenders*; *The Bill*, *London's Burning* and *Anderson* (Channel 4). Theatre includes: *Oliver* (West End).

Company

Suzy Almond, *Writer*

Suzy was the winner of the 1997 Westminster Prize and one of six writers on the first year of Soho Theatre Writers' Attachment Programme. Her Play *The Blah Blah Kid* (a joint commission from the BBC and Soho) was broadcast on Radio 4 in February 2000. Suzy is member of Lightning Ensemble Theatre Company.

Nick Blount, *Sound Design*

Nick has been involved in Soho Theatre Company since 1996, and has been sound technician on many of the company's in-house productions, including the under 11s' showcase at Soho Theatre in 2000.

Chris Hoban, *Composer*

Chris studied music at Edinburgh University, where he began songwriting and theatrical composition. He has worked overseas concurrently as a Musical Director for British Council projects and as a teacher, living and working in Brazil, Africa, Australia and New Zealand. Aside from theatre, he composes for film including *Secondhand* (winner at Cannes in 1999) and audio books; most recently Jenny Colgan's bestseller *Amanda's Wedding*.

Luke Hunt, *Designer*

Trained at the University of Central England in Birmingham. Previous designs include *Jump Mr Malinoff, Jump* (Soho Theatre), which was a prizewinning commission in the 1999 Linbury Prize for Stage Design. Assistant designer for Richard Hudson on several operas.

Jonathan Lloyd, *Director*

Currently Associate Director at Soho Theatre where he has directed *Hunting for Dragons*; *Hey Hey Good Looking*; *Jump Mr Malinoff, Jump*; *The Backroom*; *Belle Fontaine* and *Skeleton* and run writers' workshops and the Under-11s Playwriting Scheme. Other productions include *The Backroom* (Bush); *Perpetua* (Birmingham Rep); *Summer Begins* (RNT Studio / Donmar); Channel Four Sitcom Festival (Riverside Studios); *Serving It Up* (Bush); *Blood Knot* (Gate) and *Function of the Orgasm* (Finborough). As a writer for children's television; *Dog and Duck* (ITV) and *You Do Too* (Nick Junior).

Jonathan Rouse, *Lighting Designer*

This will be Jonathan's second lighting design at Soho, his last one being *All Word's for Sex* by Jules Leyser for International Artistes. Jonathan also lights our 'Soho Nights' late night comedy events. Previous credits include: *Thark*; *Dancing at Lughnasa*; *True Dare Kiss*; *The 1999 Prizefights* (RADA); *An Audience with Murray Walker and Friends*; *Jo Brand* and *The Bert Kaempfert Orchestra* (Tivoli Theatre, Wimborne).

Soho Theatre and Writers' Centre

Bars and Restaurant

The main theatre bar is located in Café Lazeez Brasserie on the Ground Floor. The Gordon's Terrace serves *Gordon's* ® Gin and Tonic and a range of soft drinks and wine. Reservations for the Café Lazeez restaurant can be made on 020 7434 9393.

Free Mailing List

Join our mailing list by contacting the Box Office on 020 7478 0100 or email us at mail@sohotheatre.com for regular online information.

Hiring the Theatre

Soho Theatre and Writers' Centre has a range of rooms and spaces for hire. Please contact the theatre managers on 020 7287 5060 or email hires@sohotheatre.com for further details.

Also at Soho Theatre and Writers' Centre

Coming Up

24 July – 18 August
The Shagaround
by Maggie Nevill
directed by Patrick Sandford
designed by Juliet Shillingford
lighting by David W Kidd
A Nuffield Theatre, Southampton and Warehouse Theatre Croydon production of the new comedy starring Luisa Bradshaw-White and Toyah Wilcox. Selected from the 1999 International Playwriting Festival.

AT THE INTERNATIONAL EDINBURGH FESTIVAL
Previews Friday 10 and Saturday 11 August at 10pm
Performances 13–18 August at 10pm
Office
by Shan Khan
directed by Abigail Morris
Soho Theatre Company's debut at the Edinburgh International Festival with the winner of this year's Verity Bargate Award.
Edinburgh tickets and information available from:
www. eif.co.uk   0131 473 2000
Transfers to Soho Theatre from 22 August – 8 September.

soho nights

Wednesdays 27 June, 4, 11, and 18 July at 9.30pm
Cyderdelic
Devon's top dance act and committed but naïve eco-warriors, as seen on the 11 o'clock show. Reclaim the Beats!
'Fantastically innovative and astonishingly funny.' ***** The List
'Easily the most ambitious and hilarious show this year' Independent
Tickets £10 (£8 discounts)

5-7 July; 12-14 July; 19-20 July at 9.30pm
Brothers Marquez
Immaculately observed and brilliantly performed character comedy by two real brothers. See London's hottest double act prior to their TV debut – all previous Soho dates have been total sell outs.
Tickets £10 (£8 discounts)

Soho Theatre Company

Artistic Director: Abigail Morris
Assistant to Artistic Director: Sarah Addison

Administrative Producer: Mark Godfrey
Assistant to Administrative Producer: Tim Whitehead

Literary Manager: Paul Sirett
Literary Officer: Jo Ingham
Associate Director: Jonathan Lloyd
Associate Director: Mark Brickman
Director of Writers' Programme: Lin Coghlan (part-time)
Director of Young Writers' Programme: Lisa Goldman (part-time)

Development Director: Carole Winter
Development Manager: Kate Mitchell
Development Officer: Gayle Rogers

Marketing Manager: Louise Chantal
Press Officer: Angela Dias (020 7478 0142)
Marketing and Development Assistant: Ruth Waters

General Manager: Catherine Thornborrow
Front of House and Building Manager: Anne Mosley
Financial Controller: Kevin Dunn
Accounts: Elva Tehan
Finance Assistant: Hakim Oreagba

Box Office Manager: Kate Truefitt
Box Office Assistant: Steve Lock
Box Office Casual staff: Steven Egan, Leah Read, Danielle Taylor, Barry Wilson
Duty Managers: James Neville and Keith Lodwick
Front of House staff: Morag Brownlie, Ryan Clifford, Sharon Degen, Megan Fisher, Claire Fowler, Mary Green, Sarah Gurcel, Matthew Hurt, Sam Laydon, Kristina Moller-Tsakonas, Kellie Willson and Claire Townend.

Production Manager: Nick Ferguson
Chief Technician: Nick Blount
Deputy Chief Technician: Jonathan Rouse

Board
David Aukin *chair*
Cllr Robert Davis *vice chair*
Lisa Bryer
Tony Elliott
Barbara Follett MP
Bruce Hyman
Lynne Kirwin
David Pelham
Tony Marchant
Michael Naughton
Philippe Sands
Eric H. Senat
Meera Syal
Richard Wilson OBE
Roger Wingate
Marc Vlessing

Honorary Patrons
Bob Hoskins *president*
Peter Brook CBE
Simon Callow
Sir Richard Eyre

Development Committee
Lisa Bryer *chair*
David Aukin
Don Black OBE
Cllr Robert Davis
David Day
Amanda Eliasch
Catherine Fehler
Emma Freud
Madeleine Hamel
Bruce Hyman
Isabelle Laurent
Lise Mayer
Michael Naughton
Philippe Sands
Barbara Stone
Richard Wilson OBE

THE SOHO THEATRE DEVELOPMENT CAMPAIGN

Soho Theatre Company receives core funding from Westminster City Council and London Arts. However, in order to provide as diverse a programme as possible and expand our audience development and outreach work, we rely upon additional support. Many projects are only made possible by donations from trusts, foundations and individuals and corporate involvement.

All our major sponsors share a common commitment to developing new areas of activity with the arts and with the assistance of Arts and Business New Partners, encouraging a creative partnership with the sponsors and their employees. This translates into special ticket offers, creative writing workshops, innovative PR campaigns and hospitality events.

The **New Voices** annual membership scheme is for people who care about new writing and the future of theatre. There are various levels to suit all – for further information, please visit our website at www.sohotheatre.com/newvoices

Our new **Studio Seats** campaign is to raise money and support for the vital and unique work that goes on behind the scenes at Soho Theatre. Alongside reading and assessing over 2000 scripts a year, we also work intensively with writers through workshops, showcases, writers' discussion nights and rehearsed readings. For only £300 you can take a seat in the Education and Development Studio to support this crucial work.

If you would like to help, or have any questions, please contact the development department on 020 7287 5060 or at development@sohotheatre.com

We are immensely grateful to all of our sponsors and donors for their support and commitment.

SUPPORTED BY
CITY OF
WESTMINSTER

LONDON ARTS

PROGRAMME SUPPORTERS

Principal sponsors: **Bloomberg**   TBWA\GGT DIRECT

TBWA\GGT DIRECT and Soho Theatre Company have received an investment from the Arts and Business New Partners scheme to further develop their creative partnership. Arts and Business New Partners is funded by the Arts Council of England and the Department for Culture, Media and Sport.

SOHO THEATRE + WRITERS' CENTRE

In 1996, Soho Theatre Company was awarded an £8 million Lottery grant from the Arts Council of England to help create the Soho Theatre + Writers' Centre. An additional £2.6 million in matching funds was raised and over 500 donors supported the capital appeal. The full list of supporters is displayed on our website at www.sohotheatre.com/thanks.htm

BUILDING SUPPORTERS

Supported by the Arts Council of England with National Lottery funds

The Lorenz Auditorium supported by Carol and Alan Lorenz

Principal sponsor: stone

Rooms: Gordon's Terrace supported by Gordon's Gin • The Education and Development Studio supported by the Foundation for Sport and the Arts • Equity Trust Fund Green Room • The Vicky Arenson Writers' Seminar Room • Writers' Room supported by The Samuel Goldwyn Foundation • Unity Theatre Writers' Room • Writers' Room supported by Nick Hornby and Annette Lynton Mason • The Marchpole Dressing Room • Wardrobe supported by Angels the Costumiers • The Peter Sontar Production Office • The White Light Control Room • The Strand Dimmer Room • The Dennis Selinger Meeting Room

Ivory Productions Ltd • Paula Milne • Jeremy and Hilary Mogford • William Morris Agency (UK) Ltd • The Moving Picture Company • Sandra and Aharon Nathan • Trevor Nunn • Olswang • David and Liz Parfitt • Peters Fraser and Dunlop • Anthony Pye-Jeary • The Really Useful Group • Red Rooster Film and Television Entertainment Ltd • ROSC Theatre • Jan Roy • Settlement 369 Trust • Jonathan Shalit • John Sharp • Tom Stoppard • Trudie Styler • Thin Man Films Ltd • Tiger Aspect Productions • Michael Treichl Esq • Warner Bros • Sir Douglas Wass

Seats: Andy Armitage • Lady Becher • Hettie and Simon Biber • Robert Bieber • Don Black OBE and Shirley Black • Michael Black and Julie Rogers • Miron Blumental • Jules Boardman • Peter Boita • Leslie and Harold Bolsom • Graham Bradstreet • Julie and Robert Breckman • Eleanor Bron • Joy and Lionel Bryer • Tony and Barbara Buckley • Joolia Cappleman • Jos and Marny Chambers • John Chichester • Susan Coe • David and Ruth Coffer • Sylvia Coleman • Steven R Collins • Howard Cooke Associates • Christopher Corbin • Ann and John Davies • Henry and Suzanne Davis • Amanda Eliasch • Susan Ensign • Helen Fielding • Michael Frayn • Susan Frewin • Liz and Rowland Gee • Nigel Gee • Pam and Keith Gems • Anthony Georgiadis • Lord and Lady Hanson • Maurice and Irene Hatter • Tony Haygarth • Peter Hodes • Mandy Isaacs • Angela Jackson • Roslyn and Stephen Kalman • Tim and Kit Kemp • Jeremy King and Debra Hauer • Lionel and Sheila King Lassman • Peter and Lesley King-Lewis • Jonathan and Debbie Klein • Helen Kokkinou • Sara and David Kyte • Hugh and Stecia Laddie • Andria and Jonathan Lass • Colin Leventhal and Trea Hoving • Adele and Geoffrey Lewis • Lipitch Family • Paul and Paula Marber • Anthony and Pauline Margo • Valerie and Daniel Martineau • Martin and Jennifer Melman • Mark Mishon • Philip Mishon OBE and Judith Mishon • Lily and Martin Mitchell • Audrey and Geoffrey Morris • Stephen Murray • Madelaine Newton and Kevin Whately • Ossey Osmond and Roni Kermode • Joel and Merle Osrin • David Pelham • Michael Pemberton Jnr • Terence Pentony • Jill and Robin Phillips • Piper Smith & Basham • Alexander S Rosen and Armand Azoulay • Philippe Sands • Greta Scacchi • Eric and Linda Senat • John Sessions • Ingrid Simler and John Bernstein • Charlie and Jacqui Spicer • Howard Strowman • Clive Swift • Dan Tana • Norma and Brian Taylor • AP Watt Ltd • Sarah and Peter Wenban • Valerie West • Michael and Gerti Wilford • Marilyn and Geoffrey Wilson • Michael Winner Ltd • Jeremy Zimmermann

Registered Charity: 267234

First published in 2001 by Oberon Books Ltd.
(incorporating Absolute Classics)
521 Caledonian Road, London N7 9RH
Tel: 020 7607 3637 / Fax: 020 7607 3629
e-mail: oberon.books@btinternet.com

A catalogue record for this book is available from the British
Library.

ISBN: 1 84002 237 X

Cover photograph: (Brooke Kinsella in *School Play*) Stuart Colwill

Cover design: Humphrey Gudgeon

Series Design: Richard Doust

Printed in Great Britain by Antony Rowe Ltd, Reading.

ACKNOWLEDGEMENTS

Thanks to Soho Theatre for being a home from home. Special thanks to Lin Coghlan, Jonathan Lloyd and Paul Sirett for helping me with my homework.

Big thanks also to: Sarah Craig, Clare French, Cathy King, Clare Longhurst, Erin & Scott, Abigail Morris, Alison Newman, Sophie Paul, Craig Snelling, Sam Spruell, Glen Supple, Phil Temple, Lee Turnbull, Thurle Wright, that lot on the Writers' Attachment Programme (Chris Chibnall, John Corwin, Marta Emmitt, Holly Phillips, Trevor Williams), and the Soho cast (Bryan Dick, Brooke Kinsella, Tracy-Ann Oberman, Daniel Scott-Croxford).

The text is accurate to the seventh day of rehearsal.

For Stretch and Pinhead

Characters

CHARLIE
fifteen

PAUL
fifteen

LEE
fifteen

MISS FRY
thirties

Scene 1

The backstage/front of stage area of a school hall. The sounds of a music lesson going on in the room behind – piano scales or the odd burst of badly played trumpet. This is the lesser used hall in an older, more neglected part of the school. There are signs that the stage area is being used temporarily as a classroom/detention room for small numbers of pupils – some desks and chairs are still out, but most are stacked untidily at the sides, poking out from behind the curtains. There is half-light, dust and a thin beam of light from a small window. There are heavy, dusty, velvet curtains falling down, piles of costumes, wigs and props. There are small traces of set design for Peter Pan – a treasure chest, part of a pirate ship backdrop. Amongst the rubble, a piano sits, stage left.

A loud bang, the sound of a firework/banger goes off in the distance. Pause. The sound of PAUL running down the corridor. He enters, with an unlit firework still in his hand, gasping for breath. CHARLIE comes running in.

PAUL: I can't see.

CHARLIE: You screwed up.

PAUL: I can't see.

CHARLIE: You can.

PAUL: I can't.

CHARLIE: Try opening your eyes.

PAUL: Yours went off in my face.

CHARLIE: You'd already run away.

PAUL: You didn't let go.

CHARLIE: That's the idea. I only let go of it when it had burned down to the end, as close to my skin as possible, then I lobbed it right through the window. That's what you were supposed to do with yours.

PAUL: It could of exploded in your face, it was…

CHARLIE: Mine didn't explode big enough. It should have made something catch light. And there were no staff in there. What happened to yours?

She grabs PAUL's firework.

PAUL: It didn't go off, I think you'll find.

CHARLIE: You didn't light it. You're such a girl.

PAUL: I think you'll find…

CHARLIE: Stop repeating yourself.

PAUL: Last time…

CHARLIE: You're pathetic.

PAUL: I think…

CHARLIE: You've gotta have a skill if you wanna be a Hollister Boy. You've gotta push things to the limit.

PAUL: Yesterday, I got inside McGibney's head after fifteen seconds of coming into class, I think you'll find. Just sitting down, everyone's going 'Go on then, Paul.' I goes 'Sir' and I've got this Muller yoghurt blob on Dwayne's ruler and it's strawberry and it's poised and *everyone* is thinking – *no way*. Cos it's McGibney. But I think you'll find that I don't care. He turns round and I goes 'Happy Birthday Sir' – it's not even his birthday – it just made it more funnier – and I pulled back the end of the ruler – I pulled it back with *skill* – it was *skilful,* and I let it go. Slow motion pink blob leaving launch pad now. Splat on McGibney's snooker glasses what are too big for his face. He makes this squeaking noise like a hamster, I goes to *everyone* 'he sounds like a hamster.' He goes 'Paul Gibbs!' I goes 'What?' I should of took a stopwatch. Fifteen seconds!

CHARLIE: 'Yoghurt'? That's not a skill.

PAUL: I've got witnesses.

CHARLIE: You've gotta make them wanna know what's going on in your head.

PAUL: Betts and Driscoll were there.

CHARLIE: Betts plays the trombone, Driscoll's bottom lip is always wet.

PAUL: (*Walking out.*) I might go music.

CHARLIE: What?

PAUL: New teacher's hot, Miss Fry. She's hot, that's why. She's saying we can play CDs in class. Dwayne says she's got nipples like Volvo wheel hubs.

CHARLIE: I heard she's crap. Comes in hung-over. Someone broke the small window in B12 before it got burned down and she pretended not to notice.

PAUL: Dwayne gets to see her in his road. She lives with her parents, man. But she's got these…

CHARLIE: Go Music then. Lee Coulson will be here in a minute.

PAUL: Lee Coulson? He's been excluded.

CHARLIE: Suspended. He's back.

PAUL: He don't come in.

CHARLIE: He has today, off you go.

PAUL: He's mental. He got Colin's brother in a headlock for about five minutes and after that he had to wear a dog collar. Lee Coulson.

CHARLIE: A surgical collar.

PAUL: …For about two months. He couldn't turn his head around, people had to help him across the road, I think you'll find. Lee Coulson. And he's got a skill – He drinks milk and makes it come out his ears. Nearly got on telly for it.

CHARLIE: He wants to be a Hollister Kid. He wants in on the bike.

PAUL: You're saying no to everyone, it's just me and you.

CHARLIE: There should be a core of three.

PAUL: Course. You been working on it?

CHARLIE: Twenty questions. It can do two hundred miles an hour, but you'd get done. It's shaped to fit you, so you fly when you're on it, like you're shot from a gun. It's got two superchargers, four carburettors and nitrous bottles.

PAUL: What's that?

CHARLIE: Accessories.

PAUL: It's big innit?

CHARLIE: Massive. Nineteen fifties style, black and chrome, you know the score. There's nothing else like it in this country, cos/a one off...

PAUL: ...a one off is a one off.

CHARLIE: When you put your foot down, to someone passing, you're a flash of chrome, a blur. And when you look up close you see more details, so it works on all perspectives. Other bikes are bikes, but this one is royalty. People on The Hollister Route will stand and stare – as we ride through the town, circling the monument, taking it slow, so by the time we hit the high street they'll be lining up outside World of Windows with their hands on their hips and their mouths wide open. You make your mark on any bike, but when it's a customised Hollister...

LEE enters.

LEE: It's only a bike.

PAUL: Lee. Nice one, you're back.

LEE: You a year ten?

PAUL: No, eleven. The older end. The pair of us are doing detention in here tomorrow night. Ten sessions cos of Mrs Glossop's breakdown, she went off the railtracks.

LEE not impressed.

Basically that was our doings.

CHARLIE: She was only a boss-eyed supply. We gave her a twitch, it come on slow.

PAUL: She lost it.

CHARLIE: Two weeks. Not our record.

PAUL: Half a day, Mr Chalamaine.

CHARLIE: One day: I count Stewart, Philips and the chinless one.

PAUL: Two days: I count Glennister.

CHARLIE: …and Burgess.

PAUL: Philips bent down to pick up the board wipe and just never got up.

CHARLIE: I like getting under people's skin.

LEE: So I've heard.

CHARLIE: (*To LEE.*) Just a bike?

LEE: Yeah.

CHARLIE: I don't think so.

LEE: No?

CHARLIE: This is about riding on a reputation.

LEE: I can do that on my own.

CHARLIE: Then why d'you bother showing up?

PAUL: Yeah.

Pause.

LEE: Sniffing it out. Stinks in here. Can still smell the charcoal from B12.

CHARLIE: John Briggs told me he was gonna torch it well before he did it. Told me when I brought him back to mine.

LEE: Briggsy?

CHARLIE: I had him outside my garage, he likes doing it in the open air. After, he was trying to get a look of the bike, but the window's all frosted up, and I wouldn't let him see it anyway. So he's looking at the window, like he's hypnotised. The wind's making the door creak, it's pitch black and the hair on the back of his neck is up. I'm like 'you okay, John Briggs?' He can't get his fag in his mouth quick enough, looking for his matches and digging deep in the wrong pocket for ages. 'Yeah', he goes.

Beat.

Yeah, right.

Beat.

After a couple of minutes…

Pause. The music behind becomes clearer. Trumpet scales.

LEE: Listen to that shit.

PAUL: (*To CHARLIE.*) Did he see it?

CHARLIE: Course not. (*To LEE.*) Finney of the Fat Lip. That's what a brass instrument does to your face. I hate that sort of music.

LEE: Lips like a sink plunger. He needs the rest of his face sorting out to match.

PAUL: I know, I know, he's weird! He ain't got a telly, you can't talk to him!

LEE: Wandering round town with the St Hilda's girl, they've both got the same coats, I says 'You're a joke, music boy.' This was in the loo. I'm like slam, Finney, your face suits the wall. And I wish I could bottle the look on his face.

PAUL: Is it true you got expelled from St George's for hitting that teacher?

LEE: Slam, Paul, Slam!

PAUL: Ha ha!

CHARLIE: (*Mocking.*) 'Slam.' Not just teachers with me. I've just messed up Rachel Perriman's head. Her and Donna Underwood have been trying to undermine me and my name. I let it go until last week double maths, when I told her I'd had Ben Cornell, who she's been seeing for six months. Except I never actually told her, I just come in with his best coat on, he lent it me. Same as blacking her eye.

PAUL: She's nice.

CHARLIE: She's not.

PAUL: (*To LEE.*) Didn't you play at her party? Do a turn on the decks?

LEE: Er...No.

PAUL: You're a DJ...innit?

LEE: Wrong man. Yo Mr DJ. Check it out! Er...no.

PAUL: Check it out! Yo school disco! This one goes out to the massive crew in the staffroom. Bo selecta! That would have been your second skill, underneath the milk one.

LEE not impressed.

CHARLIE: I'm doing her up.

LEE: So I hear.

CHARLIE: We're gonna do the original Hollister Route. Speed through town, and not get caught.

LEE: I think we should include the car park.

CHARLIE: It's not on The Route.

LEE: It should be. If you want the right people to see it.

PAUL: Yeah, Lee, totally. Did you hear about McGibney and the Muller Yoghurt?

LEE: McGibney in a sex scandal? Nice one.

CHARLIE: Paul. (*To LEE.*) Telling me a new start to the route, you're not even bringing a bike. Even Paul's bringing a bike, yeah it's shit but...

PAUL: Er...

LEE: You think you've got any clout, just the pair of you?

CHARLIE: You don't supply *all* the attitude. And there's a queue.

LEE: And they can all ride?

Pause.

CHARLIE: (*To LEE.*) 'Staring me out.'

LEE: You're in the way of what I'm looking at.

CHARLIE: You know what I wanna see? I wanna see...

LEE: I wanna see if you're capable of heading this up.

PAUL: (*To LEE.*) I wouldn't be here.

Pause.

CHARLIE: We start from the back gate.

PAUL: The original Hollister Boys started from there.

CHARLIE: (*To LEE.*) And...?

LEE: I know the score.

CHARLIE: They walked across the school field, there was a core of three.

PAUL: They should have been in class, but they were better than that. They'd show up, be seen…

CHARLIE: …and then leave. Like a swarm. If the sun was out, there was a shape behind them, a shadow. You looked out the window and they was always heading towards the back gates. If a teacher was behind them, chasing, they'd slow down to a crawl, and then so did the teacher, cos they didn't really wanna catch up with them.

PAUL: The bikes were parked at the gates. There were two or three.

CHARLIE: But only one was a Hollister. And that was at the front. The ones who didn't have them sat on the back.

PAUL: If they was lucky enough.

CHARLIE: Kids from St Georges and Fairview were hanging around, desperate for a ride. But they wouldn't ask. You had to wait to be asked. And then they drove along The Route, and The Route is always the same. We're slow at the start…

PAUL: …Taking in the scenery.

CHARLIE: The one on the Hollister sets the pace. We keep it as a slow burn for as long we can. And every corner you turn, people are staring at that lead bike. We save the best till last and force a fuck-off sound when we shoot past the police station.

PAUL: Licence? Er…no.

CHARLIE: If they put up a chase…

PAUL: It gets fun, you put your foot down.

CHARLIE: …and you all start shouting above the noise of the engines and it's like a hum, like a crowd coming in from two towns away, riding on the same note and it just gets louder. Until it arrives and then it's a roar.

Pause.

Let's go for Thursday. Meet you at the back gates.

LEE: Not the best day for me.

CHARLIE: Meet you at the car park.

LEE: Might have something on, but...

CHARLIE: Change your plans.

LEE: Click your fingers, who are you?

Pause.

CHARLIE: What else is there to do?

Pause.

LEE: You might see me.

CHARLIE: Paul?

PAUL: You might see me. You probably definitely will.

Scene 2

The stage, the following afternoon. CHARLIE lying on the floor, looking injured. PAUL beside her, on the lookout, deciding how to lay a piece of debris over her.

PAUL: D'you think she's forgotten?

CHARLIE: Yeah. Five minutes and then I'm going. I need to get back and work on the bike.

PAUL: She might have had to keep her own class behind.

CHARLIE: She's round the back of the swimming pool, having a fag. I saw her twenty minutes ago.

PAUL: Yeah?

CHARLIE: With her jumper covered in cat hair. She don't even get dressed up for school. I bet she stinks, man.

PAUL: She won't buy this.

CHARLIE: She will, she'll freak out cos it's her fault for leaving us unattended.

PAUL: Your breath smells.

CHARLIE: Don't come so close then.

PAUL: No, it don't smell too bad. It's sweet.

CHARLIE: Don't come so close.

PAUL: I'm supposed to be looking after you.

CHARLIE: Don't get too into it.

PAUL: You don't fancy a snog then?

CHARLIE: You're grossing me out.

PAUL: Joke. You got no depth in your humour.

CHARLIE: Where is she? She can't be bothered.

PAUL: I went this morning, but it was just a bit of clapping to CDs, cos she couldn't find the key to the book cupboard.

CHARLIE: Make out it's my back, okay? So don't go saying 'miss, she hurt her leg.'

PAUL: You reckon Lee will come Thursday?

CHARLIE: Course, he wants Danny Chapel and the Fairview lot to see he's got a bike. You better smarten up your bike, I don't want an embarrassment behind me.

PAUL: He could ride mine and I could ride yours.

CHARLIE: I can ride.

Beat.

But I might let him ride mine to start with and I'll go on the back, depends on my mood.

PAUL: You're all over Lee.

CHARLIE: Get a life.

PAUL: Like a bad rash, you go weird.

CHARLIE: He's a lard-ass, bong-eyed.

PAUL: She's coming.

MISS FRY comes rushing in, looking flustered.

MISS FRY: Right, let's get a move on, pull those chairs out, no nonsense…(*Seeing her.*) Fuck it!

PAUL: She just fell.

CHARLIE: Miss, I can't move.

PAUL: She can't move, miss.

MISS FRY: What were you told about messing around in here?

CHARLIE: Not to.

PAUL: Not to. She was prancing and dancing and she just tripped.

CHARLIE: And fell from up there. I brought the pole down. Aargh!

MISS FRY: What hurts…what have you done?

CHARLIE: Fucked it right up. That's what I've done. I'm panicking! I can't breathe, miss!

MISS FRY: Go and get a teacher.

PAUL: What, now?

MISS FRY: Go on you idiot.

PAUL stands at the back, watching.

What were you doing?

CHARLIE: Mucking about on the balcony.

MISS FRY: Is it your leg?

28

CHARLIE: My back. It feels like...ah...my spine or something.

MISS FRY: Stay still, do not even attempt to move... (*To PAUL.*) I said go and get a teacher.

CHARLIE: Breath deeply miss, I bet it's nothing. Aaah!!!

MISS FRY: Keep still.

CHARLIE: You better go and get the teacher, miss, he's useless.

MISS FRY: Are you... Oh God keep still. (*She turns around and sees PAUL laughing.*) Is this a joke?

CHARLIE: Sorry about that, miss. But you did leave us unattended.

PAUL: You did leave us unattended, miss.

MISS FRY: This is not fucking funny. You scared the shit out of me.

CHARLIE: Easy with the language, miss.

MISS FRY: Go and sit down.

CHARLIE: Miss.

PAUL: I'm going now, miss. Can I go?

MISS FRY: Now! Both of you!

CHARLIE: What do you expect if you're late?

MISS FRY: Shut up the pair of you...

CHARLIE: Miss.

MISS FRY: I won't say it again, shut up.

CHARLIE: You just did.

PAUL: You said it again.

MISS FRY: Do you want another ten detentions? Or I can stand you in the corner for an hour.

Pause.

Right, we've got to sort out this mess in here this week. This place has got to be fit for some of the music lessons and detentions, until B12 has been refurbished.

CHARLIE: I know who done it.

MISS FRY: ...and I don't *care* who *done* it, I just want it clean and I want it done now, we've got the next school production to clear up for.

PAUL: We don't have school productions.

MISS FRY: You do now, it's part of the department's new brief.

CHARLIE: Cos there's going to be an inspection by the authorities.

PAUL: (*To CHARLIE.*) I'd like to see her brief.

CHARLIE: Making us stand for an hour, we could do you under human rights abuse.

MISS FRY: Well, it's my right to be a sadist. (*Handing them dusters and polish.*) You mermaid. You waves. Don't miss bits, don't skimp with the polish, elbow grease isn't something that comes in a tin. Start.

CHARLIE: I thought it did miss, same as stripey paint.

PAUL: Hee hee!

CHARLIE: The cleaners should be doing this.

MISS FRY: I said start.

CHARLIE and PAUL are cleaning but keep getting distracted by the possibilities with props.

MISS FRY: What are you doing with that cloth, put that sword down.

CHARLIE: How is this teaching us about music?

MISS FRY: It's a punishment, get on with it.

PAUL: (*To CHARLIE.*) You mad, I like all this running around?

CHARLIE: I don't wanna clean props that aren't gonna be used. There's not gonna be a school play – you'd have to have five understudies for the drama teacher. Ha ha!

PAUL: Ho ho!

CHARLIE: Hee hee!

PAUL: Tee hee!

They are now having a sword fight.

MISS FRY: Do you realise how pathetic you both look?

CHARLIE: We're fifteen.

PAUL: We've got an excuse.

MISS FRY: Put them down, now!

They carry on.

CHARLIE: Stab ya!

PAUL: Stab ya!

MISS FRY: Are you listening to me?

CHARLIE: Stab ya!

PAUL: Stab ya!

CHARLIE: Stab ya!

MISS FRY: Actually Charlie's right.

CHARLIE: Yeah?

MISS FRY: Let's do some work.

PAUL: Not work.

MISS FRY: Dusters down. We'll look at composers and composition.

PAUL: (*To CHARLIE.*) Well done, you spasticated farm animal.

CHARLIE: I hate composers. Drawing snowmen on staves.

MISS FRY: Put them down.

PAUL: I want to clean the swords. I like weapons.

MISS FRY: Sort out the desks, sit down, books out.

CHARLIE: Forgot my books.

PAUL: No books, me neither.

CHARLIE: Can I please play the new piano miss?

MISS FRY: Leave it.

CHARLIE: I can play.

MISS FRY: I said leave it.

CHARLIE sits down at the piano and prepares to play like a Maestro.

MISS FRY: If I have to drag you by the scruff of the neck…

CHARLIE: You can't touch me.

A pause and then she hammers the keys, singing/shouting:

Mrs Glossop was a prat
Mr Reilly was a twat
They looked like they'd been shat
Out of somebody's arse.

PAUL claps.

MISS FRY: No surprises there, then.

CHARLIE: Meaning?

Pause.

MISS FRY: Let's get on with the Mozart work you're missing in class, take these, read.

She hands out papers. CHARLIE is now completely resistant, pushing the paper off the desk. MISS FRY sits at the piano and starts to play a personal piece that she's obviously having difficulties with.

PAUL: (*Turning over paper.*) It's got phone numbers on it, miss.

CHARLIE: Show.

PAUL: The… Frag…

MISS FRY: Give it/here.

PAUL: …and/…

CHARLIE: (*Snatching it.*) The Frog and Princess Acoustic Rock Room. 0208…

MISS FRY: I'll take that please.

CHARLIE gives her a foul look. MISS FRY breaks the stare and continues to tussle with the bag slung over her shoulder, as she looks for the relevant paper – failing to notice contents of bag spilling out.

CHARLIE: You've dropped your B&H, miss.

PAUL: B&H to your left miss, by the stool.

MISS FRY: (*Finding it and handing it out.*) Be quiet. Read the Mozart sheet. (*She goes back to the piano and struggles again with her phrase.*) Turn your papers over, It's only a paragraph. Where did Mozart come from?

Pause.

Well?

CHARLIE: You told us to be quiet.

PAUL: This is the instruction which we are now following.

MISS FRY: Yeah, very funny. Try being as funny on your thirtieth detention, they're stacking up.

CHARLIE: This is the about the thirtieth time we've got this same worksheet.

PAUL: Yeah, the one before Glossop give us it in class.

CHARLIE: …and Glossop give us it.

PAUL: Chinless…

MISS FRY: I want some quiet.

Beat.

PAUL: (*Quietly.*) …The chinless one give us it.

MISS FRY: You should know the answer then.

CHARLIE: Salford?

MISS FRY: Close – Salzburg.

CHARLIE: Damn.

MISS FRY: What age did he start composing at?

PAUL: Five.

CHARLIE: Three.

PAUL: What?! Ha ha!

MISS FRY: He was six. Now, one of Mozart's many skills was that he had perfect pitch.

PAUL: Er…

MISS FRY: Yes, what?

PAUL: Yeah, I'll go along with that.

MISS FRY: Perfect pitch. What does it mean?

CHARLIE: It's like…Wembley or Highbury. The right number of white lines and a full time man to paint them.

PAUL: It's when you can hear the note.

MISS FRY: Almost. It's when you can hear the note perfectly. This is a gift. It is something that very few people are born with.

PAUL: Er…

MISS FRY: Yes, what?

PAUL: Yeah, I'll go along with that.

MISS FRY: It would be nurtured by finding a teacher at a young age – In his case his father, who exploited his gift with controlled and dedicated teaching during his early years.

CHARLIE: (*Reading the paper.*) Oh yeah. (*In a robot voice.*) 'He exploited his gift with controlled and dedicated teaching during his early years.'

MISS FRY: Read it aloud then, if that's what you'd like to do. When you've finished, you can copy it out five times, keep you quiet. Start from the top, John.

PAUL: My name's Paul, miss.

MISS FRY: It's a big school, Paul.

CHARLIE: Copy, John, copy.

MISS FRY turns her back on them, to listen. Pause.

MISS FRY: Come on then.

PAUL: (*Struggling.*) Wolf…Wolf…

Beat.

MISS FRY: Can you…?

CHARLIE: (*Snatching it.*) I'll do it. Wolfgang Amadeus Mozart had a remarkable talent and must rank as one of the leading composers of all time.

MISS FRY's mobile phone rings.

MISS FRY: Hang on. (*Picking it up.*) Oh hiya, thanks for calling!… I'm in a detention… Yeah, I've been a naughty girl… Yeah, I can be there, I heard your tape and I thought… I've got… Yeah, I can play that, if you want a Latino twist to it I can… Yeah, it'll be great, it sounds like the kind of band that would really... Brilliant. See you there, nice one, bye for now. (*She puts phone back in bag. Seems really 'up' now.*)

Something has been understood between PAUL and CHARLIE – they have somehow silently hatched a plan while she has been on the phone.

Right, where did we get to? Go back to the beginning again, Charlotte. (*Writing in her diary.*)

CHARLIE: Okay, miss. Off we go.

'Wolfgang Amadeus Mozart had a remarkable talent and must rank as one of the leading composers of all time. Born in 1756 in Salzburg, his musical ability surfaced at a very early age. He was composing and performing at the tender age of six. He had perfect pitch and after hearing a piece of music for the first time, he could write down all of the notes played from memory...'

During the reading, it becomes apparent that CHARLIE has started to pretend to toss PAUL off under the desk. PAUL is faking ecstasy, going cross-eyed. CHARLIE is staring at MISS FRY. When MISS FRY turns around, PAUL pretends to start tucking himself in.

MISS FRY: Put that away!! Do them up...DO THEM UP.

PAUL: It was her, miss.

CHARLIE: He made me do it.

MISS FRY: Get out of the room. It's not big and it's not clever. Out!

CHARLIE: It's not big.

MISS FRY: NOW! You are pathetic.

PAUL is shaking, he looks confused and like he's about to burst into tears.

PAUL: Why me?

MISS FRY: (*To PAUL.*) YOU – to Mr Hamill's now.

PAUL: It was in my pants the whole time.

CHARLIE: Paul, listen, you better go see Mr Hamill.

PAUL: Huh?

CHARLIE: You don't have to tell him what you did. Okay?

MISS FRY: Get out before I rip the arse-end out of you.

PAUL: Okay I'm going.

CHARLIE: I'll go instead.

MISS FRY: Sit down!

CHARLIE: Someone normally has to take him out.

MISS FRY: It's all part of the act. (*To PAUL.*) Do I have to march you there?

He exits. MISS FRY sits by the piano and starts to try and play.

CHARLIE: You in a band?

Pause.

Gonna be famous?

MISS FRY gives up on tune and gets books out to mark.

Everyone's calling you...

MISS FRY: We're here, we have to be here. Let's make the best of it by ignoring each other. (*She pulls a personal stereo out of her bag and starts to listen. She attempts to mark some books, but is distracted by the music.*)

CHARLIE: Are you with us, miss? Huh?

Scene 3

The stage. MISS FRY working out a song on the piano. Having problems with it.

MISS FRY: (*Singing.*) And you say you know… And you say… And you say you know what I mean. But whatever you say…

CHARLIE enters.

CHARLIE: Where am I supposed to sit? Detention and no chairs out.

MISS FRY: You didn't come at all last week.

CHARLIE: Thought we'd give you a break, miss. But I'm bored today. And my dad said 'You'd better go your bazooka class, or else…'

MISS FRY: Oh yeah? Well, no tooth and comb, you'll have to sit down and shut up instead.

CHARLIE: Everyone's calling you ET. Cos your neck's like a Fallopian tube and you've got a big head.

MISS FRY gives her something to read and goes back to her playing (no words this time).

MISS FRY: Questions in ten minutes.

CHARLIE: Did this last week in class.

MISS FRY: Doubt you were listening. (*She continues to play.*)

CHARLIE: Heard that Mr Hamill gave you that new piano – his personal one from home, so as you can do music club and put on a musical. We haven't done a show since *Peter Pan* when I was year seven. Heard that you're doing… *Peter Pan.* You've only gotta dust off the same props. Alright innit?

Pause.

Nice piano, though, miss.

MISS FRY: This room is going to be locked.

CHARLIE: Like someone here wants to use it anyway. How come you eat lunch on your own?

MISS FRY: It's all water off a duck's back, so I wouldn't bother.

CHARLIE: You should go before it gets dark. It's haunted in here – by the ghosts of dead teachers from hundreds of years ago. Their eyeballs are hanging out of their sockets like the legend of Manjit Sidhu's javelin accident. They wander round the gallery – moaning and sighing.

MISS FRY: No worse than year Eleven's, then. Read.

CHARLIE: It's not hard being a teacher, you just hand out photocopies.

MISS FRY continues to tinker on piano.

It's hard doing music though. Hard not to make it sound like a dog howling.

MISS FRY: There's a letter in the post to your parents.

CHARLIE: Parent.

MISS FRY starts to hum to what she's singing. CHARLIE howls like a dying animal. MISS FRY slams the piano lid down.

MISS FRY: There are people in your class who want to learn to play an instrument, and every time you open your vicious mouth you steal something from them.

CHARLIE: Did I say something?

MISS FRY: …Sarah Dunn and painfully shy Drew and that boy who sits at the back and/never says anything…

CHARLIE: …/John Cherry.

MISS FRY: I see them out of the corner of my eye – their faces lighting up when they're on the third round of Frère Jacques and they realise that the noise they are making with a knackered old xylophone and a couple of tambourines, for a split second actually sounds wonderful. And just as that second arrives, *you* come crashing in and point out that one of them might look stupid. And it all falls apart. And they may laugh along with you now, but in ten years time, when they are looking for some small release from a terrible day and they end up punching walls when they could have been singing, they will remember you and hate you. I've got work to do and so do you.

CHARLIE: It's not school work, it's *your* work. That's why he gave you the piano.

MISS FRY: Lesson over.

CHARLIE: To keep you sweet, so you can practice.

MISS FRY: You're excused.

CHARLIE: Your song's miserable, move over.

She sits next to her. MISS FRY gets up and goes over to her bag on the other side of her room, finds a phone, as CHARLIE starts to mess about again.

CHARLIE: Mrs Glossop was a prat. Mr Riley was a twat.

MISS FRY: I'm phoning the Teacher On Call, I'm not wasting any more energy on you.

CHARLIE: Gone home. (*She continues to mess about on the piano.*)

MISS FRY: I want you out of here now, did you hear me?

CHARLIE starts to play a proper melody – probably something like 'Let it Be'. MISS FRY puts the phone away and listens until she finishes the verse.

MISS FRY: Well.

CHARLIE: This place still stinks of charcoal. I should of told Briggsy not to bother.

MISS FRY: What were you doing with your hands? Show me.

CHARLIE jumps up and starts to leave.

CHARLIE: You said I could go now.

MISS FRY: Well, I might like to see some more.

CHARLIE: It's not music club.

Pause.

MISS FRY: It sounded good.

Pause.

If you came in here to prove a point…

Beat.

Big deal.

Long pause.

What else can you play?

Long pause

Well?

Beat.

This is ridiculous. I can't be…

CHARLIE starts to play something else, this time adding a few chords. Probably something like 'Take These Chains From My Heart'. She makes a lot of mistakes, stops and bangs the lid down.

CHARLIE: Cunt piano.

MISS FRY: Sit down.

CHARLIE: The keys/are wide…

MISS FRY: Sit down/

CHARLIE: It's fucking/different…

MISS FRY: Sit down.

CHARLIE: (*Sits down.*) Different from what I practice on.

MISS FRY: Okay. Let's have a look at what you've been doing.

CHARLIE messes about again.

MISS FRY: Stop wasting time.

CHARLIE: Whose time?

MISS FRY: I'm genuinely interested. Okay? Play that first chord from the second piece.

CHARLIE: Take your nose out of my end.

MISS FRY: Just the chord, nothing else.

CHARLIE plays the first chord.

Good. Do you know what the chord is called?

CHARLIE: Yeah.

Beat.

MISS FRY: What?

CHARLIE: What?

MISS FRY: The chord.

Beat.

Is G Major.

CHARLIE: I know. (*She starts to play the whole song again, attempting to be more competent.*)

MISS FRY: We won't look at that just yet. Let's go back to the first chord…Charlie.

CHARLIE carries on.

MISS FRY: We'll come back to it… First chord.

CHARLIE: I didn't finish it.

MISS FRY: First chord.

CHARLIE: We did it before.

MISS FRY: You must know that you need to repeat things in order to learn. You're quick enough on the uptake about everything else.

CHARLIE plays the chord.

Good, but you're bunching up your fingers, you're not about to go ten rounds with Tyson. Relax your wrists... that's it...good. Now...

CHARLIE starts to play the song again.

MISS FRY: Who's teaching you?

CHARLIE: No-one. I'm doing a book that I got from the loft.

MISS FRY: It's a bit early for chords – when you learn from scratch you don't start with them... Stop playing for a moment, let's talk.

CHARLIE carries on playing.

Stop for a moment, until you know which fingers to use.

CHARLIE: The ones on my hands seem to be doing the trick.

MISS FRY: Are there numbers below notes in the book you're using?

CHARLIE: I don't know. It's in my dad's book from the loft. Can I finish the tune now, please?

MISS FRY: There are things you...

CHARLIE: What are you saying?

MISS FRY: You've developed bad habits.

CHARLIE: Are you starting on me, miss?

MISS FRY: Are you interested in this?

CHARLIE: Not really, no.

Pause.

MISS FRY: Any other musicians in the family?

CHARLIE: Only the blind harmonica player. That's what my dad says, three times a day.

MISS FRY: My dad plays the spoons – after half a bottle of Jack Daniels.

Pause.

It's very hard, playing the piano. It took me ages.

CHARLIE: It's just like doing a crossword, blacks and whites.

MISS FRY: Do you enjoy listening to music?

CHARLIE: Whatever.

MISS FRY: There's a lot of theory.

CHARLIE: I can think.

MISS FRY: I'm not suggesting... It's great that you just did it off your own back.

CHARLIE: My dad's got this thing...that he...

Beat.

MISS FRY: Thing?

CHARLIE: Keyboard thing.

Pause

First there was an old guitar... that I messed about on...then my dad's got this Casio thing in the loft. He wasn't getting on with it, got a cashew nut stuck behind the D key at Christmas and told it: fuck off. I just dug it out again. The keys on it are different size to these. The things I play on it...

MISS FRY: It's great you're into it.

CHARLIE: …are things that… What I do…which is why I don't know the right fingers… I don't use the book. I just go up and down the whites and blacks and I…

MISS FRY: …get to grips with the notes.

CHARLIE: …and I try and…

MISS FRY: …teach yourself how to play,/that's great.

CHARLIE: Forget it.

MISS FRY: What?

Pause.

What's your favourite song?

CHARLIE: Crossfire – The New Booty Boys.

Pause.

What's yours?

MISS FRY: This. (*She plays the beginning of 'My Lagan Love'.*)
Where Lagan Stream sings Lullaby
There blows a lily fair
The Twilight gleam is in her eye
The night is on her hair

Something like that.

Beat.

Right, come/on lets…

CHARLIE: It sounds sort of…

CHARLIE picks out the last nine notes with one finger – she does it pretty well – taking her a few wrong tries before finding the last two notes.

MISS FRY: Yes.

CHARLIE: Is it just me or does it really smell in here?

MISS FRY: You've only got the Casio at home?

45

CHARLIE: Yeah, it's got headphones as well, so you can do isolation work.

MISS FRY: I'll teach you.

CHARLIE: You haven't got the time.

MISS FRY: There's a piano here.

CHARLIE: You're doing your stuff on it.

MISS FRY: I can do both.

CHARLIE: I'm not up my own arse enough.

MISS FRY: And I am?

CHARLIE: Yeah, but you're up there by accident. I'd be up there on purpose.

MISS FRY: We could use this detention time. I've got this hunch that the other member of the Erith Two won't turn up again.

CHARLIE: Paul's from Crayford.

MISS FRY: If anyone comes in, I'm making you help me tune it.

CHARLIE: It's not about that.

Pause.

Now and again I might.

MISS FRY: You need to commit yourself.

CHARLIE: Like you do?

Pause.

MISS FRY: There are exams you could take. That you actually have a chance of passing. I don't mean it like that, but…We need to undo some of the habits you've developed and…we might need to go backward before you can go forward. Actually it's crap at first. Because you can't play anything your friends want to hear. And practice can be so boring, the same thing every day. But there are ways of making it more interesting.

CHARLIE: Like what?

MISS FRY: You can sort of step back from it. Sometimes if you…close your eyes and visualise it differently. Look at practice as being…like a tightrope walk. You're up there, but can you maintain that balance? The wonder of it. Can I stay on?

CHARLIE: I don't wanna be in the circus.

MISS FRY: I've got to get going. You can hold your own with those boys. Tell them what you're bloody doing and don't be a coward.

CHARLIE: That's teachery.

MISS FRY: Look… Here's a spare key to this room. And one for the piano, in case you want to practise. This is a big deal.

Pause.

I can't tolerate this silent treatment, either.

CHARLIE: You want us to think, then you moan when we do.

MISS FRY exits.

You've dropped your B&H again, there's a hole in your bag, I'll see you next time.

Scene 4

LEE and PAUL in a car park early evening. Darkness. Car lights pass intermittently and shine spots onto their faces. Music is blasting out of a stereo, probably hip hop – a big, upbeat sound. LEE is facing the world, arms folded. He has distanced himself from PAUL's bike, a shabby effort. PAUL is behind, polishing the bike and buzzing. They are both caught up in the beat (PAUL more manic), each finding their own particular version of the rhythm until the song finishes.

LEE: I love that shit. It means something.

PAUL: I went to see them.

LEE: I've been to see them.

PAUL: But it was sold out, yeah, sold out.

LEE: They came out of nothing so they mean something. They could have ended up working for the Drain Doctor – playing with sink plungers all day, picking up twenty pence tips from old ladies. But no, they're making music, no-one's calling them stupid. Music for the street, from the street…battle rhymes, songs about blood and tears and fat tunes that come up through your feet and won't leave you alone. Everything you were thinking, it's like they stole it from your head when you were sleeping. You wake up and they're playing *your* song on the radio. You wake up and say how did you *know* that, man? And if some girl, or some kid in a car park said those words to me and there was no beat, no tune, what would I do? I would laugh in their face. But these guys…I mean, they could of been Drain Doctors.

PAUL: I heard Dwayne DJ on the weekend. He takes it somewhere, really up on it.

LEE: He's shit. Buys a job lot of dance crap for 50p, cos he don't know how to browse for vinyl. He's got no lyrical know-how neither. The beat is just a backdrop for people with things to say. It's not for dancing: All this breakbeats and party anthems – that's wallpaper to me.

PAUL: People were dancing.

LEE: They weren't listening.

PAUL: He done this mix…

LEE: He can't tune a radio.

   Pause.

PAUL: I wouldn't mind some decks. Yeah, yeah.

LEE: A bike does a similar trick. Puts you in a regular public arena.

PAUL: So true.

LEE: I want Danny Chapel to see this Hollister, where is she?

PAUL: Is Danny coming tonight?

LEE: I heard something.

PAUL: He still with your ex?

LEE: Get a life, he took her off my hands. Those Fairview boys have gotta make do with seconds, yeah?

PAUL: Yeah, yeah.

LEE: They're outside school gates, backing off from teachers doing duty, it's pretty funny.

PAUL: Danny's marking you.

LEE: I'm marking Danny.

PAUL: When he stares his head shakes like he's put his finger in a socket.

LEE: I'm marking him.

PAUL: His right-hand man is marking me. But if he's getting a bike…

LEE: Well it won't be a Hollister, will it? It'll be a bogstandard 50cc that his brother nicked off someone. He'll just turn up, see what we've got and drive off with his tail between his legs. Where is she?

Pause.

LEE: It's bold this Hollister, it's got a story and that.

PAUL: Yeah, yeah.

LEE: But it's better if we don't do the exact same route. We'll start from here – leave Danny for dust as we pull out.

PAUL: Yeah, we'll customise it. We won't bother with Cross Street, that sort of thing.

LEE: You can start by taking that learner plate off.

PAUL: It's meant to be a joke.

LEE: It's not a joke, it's in case you get pulled over, you muppet.

PAUL: Pulled over! I'm lobbing it Lee, just so as you know. (*He throws the learner plate away.*) There you go, boy – meet the road!

Long pause.

LEE: Her dad don't mind about the bike?

PAUL: He don't know.

LEE: He don't know it's down there?

PAUL: He might of forgotten, it just got dumped there after the accident and no one took it away. Her dad's a bit weird. Well into cheese and onion sandwiches and he only ever says to her 'put the kettle on.' That's all he says, not all, but you know.

LEE: Her brother was cool.

PAUL: Deano Silver. Cool as. My bike's got a story. No one got killed on it, but it's full of historical facts, yeah. You got a torch?

LEE: No.

PAUL: (*Studying his bike.*) I keep seeing a scuff, when the light catches it.

LEE: What are you doing?

PAUL: Sorting the scuff mark, I'm bored, got any more?

LEE: Leave it alone.

PAUL: Got any more?

LEE: Keep still.

PAUL: Calm it right down.

Long pause. A bottle of cider.

LEE: You become associated with a bike in the same way a DJ does with his sounds. You buy a bike that reflects you – mine was a one off, it was customised.

PAUL: Is that what the tattoo's all about, is that what it's all about?

LEE: Yeah, it's the same colours as my old bike.

PAUL: Nice touch, Lee.

LEE: It was white and I had a guy who does tattoos draw doves on it. Doves are for peace, you don't wanna fight unless you have to. And the less you fight, the more harder you should hit someone when you do fight. This is the philosophy of my tattooist – calls himself a Psycho Buddhist, bit different, you know. There's small fangs coming out of the doves' mouth, so this bike is a one off. I did always feel very peaceful when I put my foot down.

CHARLIE arrives.

LEE: Where is it?

PAUL: (*Patting his bike.*) It's okay, we're only…

LEE: You stupid little cow. I wanna…

PAUL: We're only one down.

LEE: How does this make me look? Eh?

CHARLIE: That bloke from the garage is still looking at it.

LEE: For a month?

CHARLIE: He's gotta…

LEE: You're fucking me about.

CHARLIE: I'll tell him not to…

LEE: Stop fucking me about.

CHARLIE: I'll tell him not to bother.

Pause.

LEE: Ask him again.

PAUL: Fairview kids keep coming by.

LEE: A bad situation. Yeah? For me to be leaning against that. (*Gesturing to PAUL's bike.*) People are gonna believe I sold them a bad pill.

CHARLIE: It gets me down, the amount of servicing. But this bloke's doing it for the love of it, so I can't hassle him. He says that cos a Hollister is so finely tuned, it takes more than spit and polish to keep it in check. Highly strung. Every nut and bolt needs to be North, East or South facing.

LEE: That's technical.

CHARLIE: You wouldn't get it if I got deep about it.

LEE: Try me. I've had a few bikes.

CHARLIE: So you keep saying.

LEE: Driving round car parks since I was ten.

CHARLIE: I need to look at the manual. Can't lug it around, it weighs a ton.

LEE: You must know some of it.

CHARLIE: It's like the bible. Even the Pope don't know it off by heart.

LEE: You're showing me up. Every time we turn up here to show this thing off…

PAUL: Danny and all the Fairview boys are saying there is no bike.

LEE: It's escalated. Do you wanna know what's happened now? People have stopped coming for a look, they've started laughing at us. Danny's saying he's gonna turn up here with his bike and...

CHARLIE: He hasn't got a bike.

LEE: He's getting his brother's hand-me-down next month.

CHARLIE: What?

PAUL: He's set a date for it for bringing it.

CHARLIE: He's what?

PAUL: Lee and me feel we're being painted into a corner.

Pause.

Where you been hiding anyway?

CHARLIE: It's drab here when it pisses down.

LEE: Drab? Where'd you pluck that one from?

PAUL: Lee's gonna be excluded, I'm next. You been going detentions?

CHARLIE: No.

LEE: Haven't you?

Beat.

CHARLIE: No.

LEE offers her some speed.

PAUL: It don't work.

CHARLIE: No thanks.

PAUL: Huh?

LEE: I'll stick it on the tab for you.

CHARLIE: Nah.

PAUL: What's up with you?

CHARLIE: Nothing.

Long pause.

PAUL: You *live* at school, my sister says.

CHARLIE: Yeah, got a bed there. King size.

PAUL: No surprise.

CHARLIE: Very funny. As it happens I'm working on the Music teacher, Miss Fry. Found the key to that posh piano in her pigeon hole. Went in there one day and wrecked it. She's getting more thick skinned in class though. The other day I spazzed out, wouldn't let her get a word in edgeways, she goes 'you're the worst pupil I've ever had to deal with.' And I'm like 'thanks for the compliment, keep 'em coming.'

LEE: She smiled at you by the back gates.

PAUL: Gave you a look.

CHARLIE: She must fancy me.

PAUL: You're going detentions though.

CHARLIE: You're not MI5, you're Paul Gibbs and I'm going detentions to take her apart. She'll be the one spazzing out in a month's time, I'm so in her head.

Pause.

LEE: King size.

Beat.

PAUL: No surprise.

Beat.

LEE: No surprise, I think you'll find.

Pause.

PAUL: I think you'll find that...

CHARLIE: (*To PAUL.*) *You* having a go at *me*? I could beat you with my hands behind my back and a head full of draw. You'd be black and blue and I'd be standing. You farm animal!

PAUL: Suck my prick and hard!

LEE: Calm it.

CHARLIE: Farm animal.

PAUL: Suck my prick and hard!

CHARLIE: Animal.

LEE: Calm it.

PAUL: There's no point fighting between us, yeah, we could be saving the energy. Hey, Lee. I've just thought of something. Killer Doves, sounds a better name, now.

LEE: The fangs are a killer touch.

PAUL: I might get one done.

LEE: Don't get a dove.

PAUL: Might get a face.

LEE: Get a dog.

PAUL: Might do.

LEE: What time McDonagh and Devenny coming tomorrow?

PAUL: I might call them. (*Gets his mobile out.*) Scroll, scroll, scroll. D, D, D. D for Devenny, yep.

CHARLIE has got her mobile out.

CHARLIE: 020 8310 17…

LEE: What?!

PAUL: That's his *old* number.

LEE: He was a foetus when he lived there.

PAUL: Ha ha!

LEE: Ho ho!

PAUL: Hee hee!

LEE: Tee hee!

Pause.

CHARLIE: I am gonna bring it. It's just this bloke's telling me it could be another month.

LEE: Just in time then. Danny's bringing his bike a month on Friday.

PAUL: You gonna fight him?

LEE: No need. We'll just do a lap of honour here in front of all his mates. Set off on the route and leave him for dust. Dignity, Paul.

PAUL: Danny Chapel. He's got no nerve endings in his neck. His head shakes all the time.

LEE: Like a pneumatic drill. He's a bonehead. He won't be remembered. Whereas, what we're doing…especially if we're changing it slightly, if we're setting up our own route, starting here. It gives us – a sparkle.

Pause.

CHARLIE: It has to be that Friday.

LEE: Getting his bike that day, cos his brother gets a new one for his birthday. He reckons it's got a fat engine. Saying he's gonna stick a sign saying Hollister Sucks on it, and tie tin cans to the back. Do a lap of honour here and then go riding round *our* Route.

CHARLIE: What?

PAUL: I'll give mine a rub down.

LEE: He fronts up a load of kids.

Long pause.

CHARLIE: Have you seen those kids? Half-wits and handicaps. We'll bring more people than you've ever seen in that car park. We'll bring more kids than even the Hollister Boys ever had tagging behind them. Don't tell me about sparkle.

PAUL: Get every single year out of our school for a look of it.

CHARLIE: Just tell them to expect something.

LEE: But not what.

PAUL: Get them going in their imagination.

CHARLIE: Ladies and Gentlemen, please join us and Danny Chapel…

PAUL: After school…

LEE: Sundown, at four.

CHARLIE: Expect his mouth open.

LEE: His jaw to hit the floor.

CHARLIE: Bring a camera.

PAUL: Say cheese!

LEE: I can do some business.

PAUL: I'll give mine a rub down.

LEE: Thinks he's a ladies man.

CHARLIE: Put your foot down…

LEE: Dust flies.

PAUL: Everyone's clapping us.

LEE: He's got a burnout of a bike.

PAUL: Lap of honour.

CHARLIE: We pull out and he's over.

Beat.

LEE: Once we press go.

CHARLIE: I know.

LEE: You can't back out.

Beat.

CHARLIE: I'm Charlie Silver.

Scene 5

The stage. CHARLIE and MISS FRY at the piano. CHARLIE is playing scales or arpeggios ploddingly. She finishes.

MISS FRY: Are you with us?

CHARLIE: (*Snapping out of it.*) Huh? Yeah, sorry miss.

MISS FRY: The examiner is going to be really impressed with you – you're doing brilliantly, Charlie.

CHARLIE: It's just I know them back to front.

MISS FRY: I know they're a bit dull.

CHARLIE: Yeah.

MISS FRY: Which is why I've been breaking up lessons with some of my favourite upbeat songs about drowning women and people who hang themselves.

CHARLIE: Don't forget the one-armed fisherman, miss.

MISS FRY: Ah, folk music.

CHARLIE: Yeah, right.

MISS FRY: Anyway it's this exam that's important – you'll feel different about a lot of things afterwards. I think it will…help you…in lots of ways.

CHARLIE: Whatever.

MISS FRY: One final session this week and you'll be ready.

CHARLIE: Thought school play rehearsals started next week. Paul's sister wants to audition for…

MISS FRY: It's been postponed. Paperwork. And I'm covering physics now. Physics. Do you know how much time I've spent writing incident reports this week? 'She spat/he broke a window/I turned around and they were gone.' Sorry, I shouldn't be telling you this. Right! The here and now – Let's look at the Minuet. What do we need to think about?

CHARLIE: (*Lacklustre.*) *Legato.*

MISS FRY: And to the ending, which needs to be…

CHARLIE: More endingly.

MISS FRY: Which needs to be…

CHARLIE: I could slow it down a bit.

MISS FRY: Come on then, dazzle me.

CHARLIE starts to play. It's not perfect, but she's concentrating.

MISS FRY: Ah, ah. What did I tell you about your wrists?

CHARLIE: Not to slit them if I get it wrong.

MISS FRY: Good, that's a lot better. Keep going.

CHARLIE continues.

Oh, hang on minute.

CHARLIE: What?

MISS FRY: Ah, ah…

CHARLIE: You're onto something.

MISS FRY: (*Taking over piano and trying things out.*) Sorry, Charlie, sorry hang on a moment. I *am* onto something. I was working on something which I couldn't resolve. It needed…it's got this lovely melancholy feel to it…and it…needs a chord on the bridge which is…going to make you…feel like… Arghh! What was in my head? Sorry. Let's get going again. Take it from the top.

CHARLIE starts to play again.

MISS FRY: Aargh. It's driving me crazy.

CHARLIE stops.

What? No… Sorry, give me two minutes.

MISS FRY plays around with a chord and starts humming.

MISS FRY: It needs…a… That's it! That's it! (*She scrabbles around for a pen and writes it down.*) Sorry about that. Fantastic, off we go. Let's pick it up again.

Pause

Charlie.

Pause.

CHARLIE roughly bangs out the three chords MISS FRY has been working on for the bridge to her song.

MISS FRY: That's my bridge.

CHARLIE: Yeah.

MISS FRY: You just played my bridge.

CHARLIE: Yeah.

MISS FRY: You've picked it up without thinking about it, that's amazing. We've done all that work on your aural skills and it's really…

CHARLIE: You know we did variations in class?

MISS FRY: Variations on a theme, yeah.

CHARLIE: You always do those three chords in the middle of the song. It's a variation. On all your other songs.

MISS FRY: It's great you're listening properly. I'm impressed.

CHARLIE: Cos it's like – you've got the same main note in the chord all the time as well.

MISS FRY: The root note…right, well not all the time, this is great, how you've come on.

CHARLIE: I would of known that anyway. It's just that now I know the word for it.

Pause.

MISS FRY: Tell me a bit more about what you did before our lessons.

CHARLIE: Stuff.

MISS FRY: What, singing?

CHARLIE: Singing!

Pause.

Listened to records, my dad don't have CDs. Some old songs like…

Beat.

MISS FRY: Like what?

CHARLIE: BB King and fat lemon jelly belly and shit like that.

MISS FRY: That stuff's really good.

CHARLIE: It's alright.

Beat.

It all sounds the same.

Beat.

Except they all have their own flavour. It sort of…

MISS FRY: It's great when…

CHARLIE: I don't mind it – like when they're howling and stuff about getting it on. My dad used to have a twelve-string guitar with a silver strap, but then he cut all the strings off with the nail scissors.

MISS FRY: Did you do anything with it?

Pause.

CHARLIE: Twenty questions. You've only got one string, there's not a lot you can do, so you...

MISS FRY: ...you'd heard those guys and you thought...

CHARLIE: So you try and think around it. Cos I can't see what they're doing with their fingers. What I did, was... I just took it and started spelling out tunes. By twisting the key at the top and pulling...not pulling...plucking the string...or I ran my fingers up and down that string and put dots where the notes were. Not dots...yeah, things were coming into my head and I'm spelling out tunes and thinking, well, I haven't heard that one before.

MISS FRY: Great. That's composition. You turn your nose up in class.

CHARLIE: Everyone's like 'You haven't got a CD player.' It's like Finney of the Fat Lip not having a telly.

MISS FRY: Did your brother play an instrument?

CHARLIE: No.

Pause.

MISS FRY: I used to play with a blues band. They were a bunch of gin soaks, but they really knew how to hold it together.

CHARLIE: Yeah?

MISS FRY: Yeah. But you've got to be able to handle it. This covers band I was with, they couldn't. Urgh they used to pour it down each other's throats on stage. I did a jazz thing and they were pretty bad, but they always waited until after. Actually the worst was the last lot –

the guy who did backing vocals was off his head – I had to turn him down oh so slowly, so he wouldn't notice.

CHARLIE: You've gotta be good to stay together. You've gotta keep eye contact and stuff. You can't be pissed.

MISS FRY: That's right. Nearly got a record deal a few times.

CHARLIE: Where have you played?

MISS FRY: All over the place – all the pubs, it's part of the deal, not very glamorous. Did a thing on a ship once. But they wouldn't let me do my own stuff. Oh, God it was awful. Now try the end of the piece again.

CHARLIE: Do you get nervous? I can't imagine playing in front of anyone.

MISS FRY: I do a bit. I get jelly legs.

CHARLIE: That's what I'll be like for the exam.

MISS FRY: It's pretty bad. Sometimes you're up on stage and you're counting the bars in your head, when you shouldn't... because it should be like breathing... I shouldn't be telling you this Charlie, it will make you more nervous about your exam.

CHARLIE: It won't.

MISS FRY: My first gig was at a place called the Running Horse. Total dive. The back of beyond, one crappy listing in the local paper, the place where old men with no teeth go to die. You psyche yourself up to imagine that this is your crowning moment, this is where it all comes together, life starts to get perfect.

CHARLIE: Bit over the top.

MISS FRY: Well, yes...and no.

CHARLIE: What was the stage like?

MISS FRY: The stage was a bit like a pen, you feel like you're about to be pelted with broken bottles or cabbages.

CHARLIE: No way!

MISS FRY: But it didn't matter because I was with my first band and it was the first time we'd had an audience. And it was kind of blessed, as a lot of first times are. It becomes more than the gig, it becomes everything. But this was always in the air, this first performance. Even when we were just sitting around after rehearsals having a drink and a laugh, we carried it with us in our mind's eye. How we would look and how the guitars caught the light and how you saved yourself for your little moment, not for what people would say when they looked at you, but for how you wouldn't be there any more. You might catch someone's eye, you might be singing to the leg of a chair at the back of the room, just seeing the varnish, the sheen of it, but you don't *know*. This was the thing with the music. You did it because you wanted to become backdrop, even to yourself. You wanted to make yourself vanish.

Pause.

Come on. *Your* piece, *your* exam.

Beat.

Once more and with feeling.

CHARLIE: It sounds like…you just let go.

MISS FRY: Yes. You should be coming to more lessons. There's so much practical stuff that you'd find fun. If you want this GCSE as well… A lot more people are turning up. I had a three-quarters full register on Thursday.

CHARLIE: I think it's more to do with your physical proportions, miss. It's not the same as *doing* it, is it? The teaching.

MISS FRY: It's just different.

CHARLIE: Mr Matheson and Miss Thomas, I can't see them doing anything else. I've tried imagining them... with a fireman's hat on, or selling newspapers, but it don't work. In their classes people hand stuff in, they keep a hush in class. Sometimes they have to work at the hush, but they keep going. When they talk about continents and the factor of ten...I believe them. But Thomas – she gets so excited – about teaching *maths,* that she's always got a rash, you know, that map of Africa on her neck.

MISS FRY: She *is* good.

CHARLIE: So I suppose...

Beat.

MISS FRY: You suppose...?

CHARLIE: I can't imagine you with a map on your neck.

MISS FRY: Not over teaching?

CHARLIE: About the music...

Beat.

...maybe. But no, not teaching.

Pause.

CHARLIE: Better get going. My dad wants a thick-cut white before the shops close. (*She starts to leave.*)

MISS FRY: Is it getting boring?

Beat.

Is it?

CHARLIE: Sometimes.

MISS FRY: Right.

CHARLIE: It's me.

MISS FRY: Well…

CHARLIE: See you, miss.

MISS FRY: Listen… Do you want to hear a version of your one-string-twelve-string on the piano?

CHARLIE: I have to get the bread, miss.

MISS FRY: I'll drop you off at the 7-11

CHARLIE: He has his sandwich at six.

MISS FRY: You're leaving half an hour early.

CHARLIE: There's a Pukka pie on the list as well.

MISS FRY: 7-11.

Pause.

Come on. We're going to make a piano sound like a guitar. (*She plays the first few chords of the twelve-bar blues.*) What's that?

CHARLIE: A chord.

MISS FRY plays some more.

MISS FRY: What is it?

CHARLIE: It's the twelve-bar blues.

MISS FRY still playing and continues to play throughout their conversation.

MISS FRY: Where does it come from?

CHARLIE: I don't know.

MISS FRY: You've done it in class.

CHARLIE: I wasn't listening.

MISS FRY: Well, just listen to it now.

CHARLIE: I don't care where it came from.

MISS FRY: What do we know about it?

CHARLIE: I can't remember.

MISS FRY: Tell me about the songs you played on the one string twelve string.

CHARLIE: I couldn't write them down.

MISS FRY: You didn't need to write them down, did you?

CHARLIE: Well I couldn't.

MISS FRY: But why didn't you need to?

CHARLIE: Huh?

MISS FRY: Why didn't you need to write them down?

CHARLIE: I dunno.

MISS FRY: Where are they now?

CHARLIE: In my head.

MISS FRY: You can't forget them?

CHARLIE: Whatever.

MISS FRY: We're going to compose now.

CHARLIE: No miss.

MISS FRY: Come on.

CHARLIE: I've gotta get the bread.

MISS FRY: Forget the bread.

CHARLIE: He can't get around, he weighs a ton.

MISS FRY: He can wait.

CHARLIE: He can't.

MISS FRY: We've got our tune.

CHARLIE: The twelve bar.

MISS FRY: We just need some words. I woke up this morning.

CHARLIE: I woke up this morning.

MISS FRY: (*Talking/building to a shout.*) I woke up this morning.

CHARLIE: (*Talking/building to a shout/then a song.*) I woke up this morning.

MISS FRY: I woke up this morning.

CHARLIE: With a song in my head.

MISS FRY: With a song in my head.

CHARLIE: It was burning a hole…

MISS FRY: It was burning a hole…

CHARLIE: Through the back of my head (I already said head!).

MISS FRY: It doesn't matter. Carry on.

CHARLIE: I was calling a boy's name.

MISS FRY: Calling a boy's name.

CHARLIE: I was punching the air.

MISS FRY: I was punching the air.

CHARLIE: Put my head out the window…

MISS FRY: Head out my window…

CHARLIE: To get some fresh air.

MISS FRY: To get some fresh air.

CHARLIE: I woke up this morning.

MISS FRY: I woke up this morning.

CHARLIE: And my heart was on FIRE.

MISS FRY: And my heart was on fire.

CHARLIE: I wanted to scream.

MISS FRY: I wanted to scream.

CHARLIE: Or drive away in a car (that I'd HIRED!)

MISS FRY: HIRED!

CHARLIE: Checked my bum for spots.

MISS FRY: Checked my bum for spots.

CHARLIE: It was clear as the day.

MISS FRY: Clear as the day.

CHARLIE: And I couldn't stop thinking…

MISS FRY: And I couldn't stop thinking…

CHARLIE: About running away.

MISS FRY: About running away.
You been so mean to me baby
So mean I can't go on.

CHARLIE: So mean, I can't go on.

MISS FRY: I gotta drink myself to death now

CHARLIE: To death now.

MISS FRY: By the end of this song

BOTH: …by the end of this song!!

MISS FRY finishes with a big flourish.

MISS FRY: Okay! Okay! That's what it's all about.

CHARLIE: Look at the state of my shoes.

MISS FRY: You little star.

CHARLIE: Mud everywhere.

MISS FRY: Well done, I feel so inspired.

CHARLIE: I've been walking around all day like a farmer.

Pause.

MISS FRY: You've done it before.

CHARLIE: Yeah. I…had some songs already. I was…you
know I was telling you about the One String…I was

making up songs before I knew what the notes were. And then I moved on to the Casio.

MISS FRY: Great.

CHARLIE: I was…making up songs even when I didn't have the guitar with me. Instead of the proper notes building up the scale – A, B, C, D etc. I would say… I would say… (*singing a scale.*) Monday, Tuesday, Wednesday, Thursday, Friday, Saturday, Sunday, Noneday. I made up quite a few songs like that. If a note went sharp or flat I'd call it Monday afternoon or Friday morning, depending. If I was out without the guitar I'd write the days down that made up my song. In case I forgot.

MISS FRY: That's amazing. I'd like to hear some of that after the exam.

CHARLIE: Okay, miss.

MISS FRY: Our final rehearsal on Friday, so don't forget to bring all your pieces with you.

CHARLIE: I can't do Friday.

MISS FRY: You need it.

CHARLIE: I'm supposed to be somewhere.

MISS FRY: It's the last session we'll get before the exam. Where do you need to be – I'll drop you off afterwards?

CHARLIE: Can't we do tomorrow?

MISS FRY: I've got bloody meetings all week. Friday. You can't do last minute practice on a Bon Tempi.

CHARLIE: A Casio.

MISS FRY: Well, whatever. All of this stuff needs commitment. It's about more than just a piece of paper. It's about…you and what you've achieved in just a few months.

Scene 6

A wall behind the car park. Darkness and spotlights. The sound of screams, cat calls and wheels screeching in the distance. PAUL and LEE come running on/climb over the wall out of breath. PAUL looks frightened and LEE's shirt is ripped.

PAUL: He lost it!

LEE: I lost it.

PAUL: I cussed him, that started it. He lost it.

LEE: I lost it. He was clinging on was all he could do.

PAUL: You could of had him.

LEE: I had him.

PAUL: His bike was like something…

LEE: He was driving a rust bucket.

PAUL: It had a fat engine, gravel was flying.

LEE: He couldn't control it…

PAUL: He kept cutting us up.

LEE: Shut up.

    Pause.

PAUL: I don't know what happened. Someone caught the back of my bike with…a stick or something, a crow bar and I done my best to grab hold of it, I done my best to grab it and use it against him…

LEE: It was a girl.

PAUL: …but I couldn't get it and he grabbed the bike and that's when you come off.

LEE: I *got* off.

PAUL: I should of pushed for *me* to ride the bike, it's my bike and I know it better than you.

LEE: It's not a bike. It's a piece of tin.

PAUL: No.

LEE: It's shit.

PAUL: ...so that was half the problem and with Danny's... Danny looked...

Long pause. They catch their breath.

LEE: Who was there? I was too engaged.

PAUL: Your ex.

LEE: Not her, who?

PAUL: Your ex and...

LEE: Who else?

PAUL: I saw a lot of faces, come for a look, they were lining up from the back door of the scout hut...

LEE: Oh, great.

PAUL: ...round the edges of the car park, there was a lot of noise, but they was a blur...a load of kids from Fairview, most of year Ten...and Eleven, McDonagh, Devenny, Rachel Perriman, Dwayne...

LEE: What?

PAUL: They changed their minds when they saw we didn't have the Hollister...they was standing with the kids from...a load of kids from Fairview. They...was cheering Danny when he arrived on his new scooter...

LEE: ...moped.

PAUL: They was cheering when he grabbed you.

LEE: Er...grabbed me, no.

PAUL: When he...when you grabbed him.

LEE: They weren't cheering.

Beat.

She blew us out.

PAUL: She must of forgot.

LEE: 'I'm Charlie Silver.' There is no bike.

PAUL: She should of come.

LEE: He's on *our* Route now, with his…

PAUL: I kept hearing the tin cans, scraping on the…

LEE: But I caught him first, I nudged his back wheel…

PAUL: I see you spin round.

LEE: I spun right round. I would have done more if I'd had some proper wheels.

Pause.

PAUL: We should go back and see who's left, get my bike.

LEE: They took it.

Pause.

PAUL: I'm not beating myself up about it.

Long pause. There is nothing to do.

Have you got anything on you, Lee?

LEE: Nothing.

PAUL: You got nothing? I wouldn't mind something.

LEE: No.

PAUL: Lee…

LEE: What's wrong with you? People kick sand in your eyes, you kick it back.

PAUL: It was all a bit weird, it was a bit of a blur. I won't go in tomorrow.

LEE: You can't anyway you muppet, you've been excluded.

PAUL: I know...I mean I nearly forgot... Nothing at all on you, Lee?

LEE exits.

Lee?

Scene 7

The stage, half an hour later. CHARLIE at the piano, playing the Minuet with concentration, humming along. LEE comes running in.

CHARLIE: What?

Pause.

LEE: Thanks.

CHARLIE: You shouldn't be...

LEE: Excuse the mess...

CHARLIE: You've been excluded.

LEE: ...I'm covered in shit, cos I got dragged...

CHARLIE: I had to be here.

LEE: ...off the back of a bike.

CHARLIE: Lee.

LEE: It was supposed to be a lap of honour, but Danny turns up with a bike twice the size of Paul's and...

Silence.

A kid tried to dunk my head in a loo when I was a Year Eight. I was the smallest boy in school then. He was big, could of drowned me, but I was too fast on my feet. I was brighter than any other bonehead cos I *needed* to be sharp twenty-four seven. And then suddenly I shot up in size, got the muscles, and I was the kick-ass kid as well as the smart one. And it got to the stage where what-I-was-all-about/my noise, walked into the room ten minutes before I did. I can't show my face. Anywhere. There is no bike.

CHARLIE: There is.

LEE: You let me down.

CHARLIE: There is, I'm telling you.

LEE: I'm a ghost now, I'm not a person.

CHARLIE: People will forget. I play the piano, I've got an exam tomorrow. I need to practice, Lee.

LEE: I know. Why'd you think I'm here?

CHARLIE: I'm into it.

LEE: It's common knowledge.

CHARLIE: I was into it well before school got a hold, this is it.

LEE: Where is she? Late?

CHARLIE: She's always exactly half an hour late.

LEE: School finished an hour ago.

CHARLIE: I get the practice, it's our thing.

LEE: Your thing.

CHARLIE: Yeah, ten minutes for her smokes, ten for her watch being out and ten…for her being her, so what? She blew my mind the other day, she…I've got a hold of it. I can't explain but…

LEE: Go on then, explain.

CHARLIE: Take the piss.

LEE: Tell me, turn me round.

CHARLIE: I shouldn't need to. You know about music. You're the DJ.

LEE: Er, DJ...no.

CHARLIE: What about Rachel's party – when you took over the decks, when you said 'this room is mine now', you made an announcement.

LEE: Er...no. It was a joke, I was pissed up.

CHARLIE: It didn't go great and cos Dwayne and Danny and some Fairview kids were there...

LEE: What is this shit-filled story of yours?

CHARLIE: Why are you denying it? I know where you're coming from. Miss Fry says that...

LEE: She's shit.

CHARLIE: She told me that.

LEE: She told me nothing. Went to her class before I was excluded – looked right through me.

CHARLIE: You were probably staring at her tits.

LEE: Excuses. You gonna be in the Philharmonic orchestra?

CHARLIE: When you do something you don't have to be the best. If everyone thought like that, there wouldn't be any buses, cos...

LEE: What?!

CHARLIE: ...cos all the bus drivers would want a Gold medal every time they pulled out the station... Not bus drivers... I mean no-one would dare look at the stars in case someone goes 'Think you're an astronaut?'... Miss Fry says...

Pause.

LEE: Miss Fry says what? Go on explain it to me, then. It had better be good, that my name got undermined.

CHARLIE: You've gotta understand...that I gave her a hard time for ages, I was so under her skin. A few years ago she got pissed up with all the bands, I thought – yeah I'll hang out with you.

LEE: And…?

CHARLIE: She was mental.

LEE: A lot of people are.

Pause.

CHARLIE: She… One lesson…you see, some lessons she didn't actually teach. And sometimes, especially at the beginning, what she did was boring, you don't wanna hear, she drones. But now and again… One time she was about to play a song about a lady who drowned in a river, but it was nothing to do with the lesson, it was just that she liked it. I said it sounds miserable to me, miss, but she said hang on, and she told me the story: It's a sad song, she said…she fought for love and she lost…and now her skin is white as a lily, her lips are rose red, she's still, and she floats downstream. She told me to close my eyes and imagine it was a dark moonlit night and that the water was lapping around the lady, taking her in. She said that when she got to the bridge of the song there would be a special note that didn't sound like the rest of the tune. It was a high sound, extra sad, a black key near the end of the piano – and when I heard it I had to imagine it was like a shooting star bursting across the river, trying to wake up the lady. I told her I couldn't be bothered, but when she started to play… And at the end of the second verse, when she hit that key and the sound broke, I felt the note shoot through the roof of this room like a bullet and I saw the star burst and I wanted the lady to wake up. I couldn't wait for that note to come round again. So that she'd open her eyes.

Pause.

LEE: Charlie.

CHARLIE: What?

LEE: (*Pulling out a piece of paper from is pocket.*) Look at this.

CHARLIE: What is it?

LEE: I used to have a white bike and I applied excellence in keeping it clean. I fought for it, I was up against the weather. Some of these teachers, they don't apply so much excellence in their day to day business, they leave things lying around. Confidential information about students. Just cos you don't have to be the best – don't mean you're allowed to be the worst.

CHARLIE: My profile, big deal.

LEE: And another internal report. It was left on the desk in the Physics room with a load of others. Paul's sister got hold of it a few days ago.

CHARLIE: 'Charlie is a bad influence on anyone who wants to learn. She is always naughty in class and has got the attention span of a gnat. Blah blah blah.' Don't give a shit, you read it.

LEE: You read it.

CHARLIE: You.

LEE: I won't read both pages, just the Miss Fry one.

CHARLIE: Both if you like, whatever.

LEE: 'Profile. Charlie Silver. Charlie is fifteen years old. Charlie's er…

CHARLIE: Read it.

LEE: Charlie's brother was killed in motorbike accident twelve months ago.'

CHARLIE: And…?

LEE: Charlie's behaviour in class is consistently aggressive. She finds it difficult to socialise with other children, particularly girls. She cannot concentrate and an incident with a fire extinguisher last year confirmed that she is...

CHARLIE: Oh yawn, I'm yawning.

LEE: ...confirmed that she is a disruptive force, to the detriment of the other children's progress.

CHARLIE: Boring. Skip the boring please.

LEE: (*Turning to next page.*) Blah blah blah... Music Report from Miss Fry... I am worried about how Charlie will react to my leaving. She has become very attached to me and I think she will find it very hard to settle into working with a new teacher. She is impatient with her practice and can be clumsy – but when her wilfulness translates into enthusiasm she tries very hard and she has recently warmed as a personality, even giving me chocolates after lessons as a thank you.

CHARLIE snatches it from him.

CHARLIE: Give it here. (*She screws it up and kicks the piano stool over.*)

LEE: Are you okay?

CHARLIE: Yeah.

LEE: I tried to tell you. I'm sorry. I mean it.

CHARLIE: I know.

LEE: I shouldn't have brought it. But she shouldn't have left it lying around. It's not just you, there's a load flying around school, they were found a few days ago, got photocopied. Charlie, she was taking you for a ride. She's a half-arsed supply teacher, making out she was a permanent. That's what they all do – they think we're stupid.

Pause.

CHARLIE: Yeah.

LEE: See?

CHARLIE: Yeah.

Long pause.

LEE: What you laughing at?

CHARLIE: The stuff in my head, that I never told you. Like that her breath stunk, man, she smelt of B&H all the time. So I'm always tipping my head away, and she goes sit up straight, not knowing why I'm leaning like the tower of Piza! And when she did her own music, it cracked me up cos she looked like a muppet, shaking like a spazzer. If I was her bloke, I would be so down on her, cos she didn't shave her legs, yeah, all the stubble coming through her tights.

LEE goes to the piano and starts to mess about.

CHARLIE: Jolly good Lee, well done, that was so inspiring. You must sit up straight. You must do more plinks.

LEE: And less plonks?

CHARLIE: Exactly. And please stop looking at my tits, and oops I'm late and fuck it, I've left the price tag on the bottom of my shoes. Two ninety-nine.

LEE: The Bumper Shoe Store?

CHARLIE: That's right, Lee – the Pikey shop. Oooh, you're a funny one, Lee. The things you say.

Pause.

LEE: I could of told you at the start that you don't learn music from a teacher. It comes from the street: Learning what joins one beat to the next. Running lyrical rings around people who think that reading and writing makes them the big I am. Classroom knocks the stuffing out of you.

CHARLIE: At the gig, did you…

LEE: That gig was all a joke.

Pause.

You weren't meant to dance to what I was playing.

Beat.

Why is everyone laughing? They're sitting there like they're better... Dwayne thinks he's playing hardcore stuff, but it was party anthems and that's shit. But Rachel and...Danny Chapel and the Fairview lot didn't know no different. You've gotta *listen* to what I play. I look up and the room is clearing out... I look down and it's all...

CHARLIE: ...the record jumps.

LEE: No, Charlie.

Beat.

No.

Beat.

Laughing idiots, I wanna bang their heads together.
I ain't never wasting my time on it again.

Pause.

CHARLIE: Did you pick it up from...

LEE: I picked it up from records, alright. And from walking through the streets and hearing how things come in and out of each other.

CHARLIE: That's what happens to me.

LEE: Yeah?

CHARLIE: Yeah.

LEE: Could be anything.

CHARLIE: Yeah it's sort of...

LEE: Weird innit?

CHARLIE: Yeah.

LEE: Can you play anything I know?

CHARLIE: Probably not… I play things like 'There we go at full gallop.'

LEE: Proves my point, see what I mean ? This galloping song…it's not coming from you.

CHARLIE: Yeah, but when I'm at home I…

LEE: Yeah, but…

CHARLIE: Yeah, but…

Beat.

Yeah, I suppose so.

Beat.

LEE: Play it then. The galloping one.

CHARLIE: Nah.

LEE: For a laugh…

Beat.

Sorry, I didn't mean…

CHARLIE: Forget it.

Pause.

LEE: I like your attitude. The way you square up to people. All the bike stuff.

CHARLIE: I don't like yours. You're such a wimp. Ha ha.

LEE: Ho ho.

CHARLIE: Hee hee.

LEE: Tee hee.

They kiss.

She'll be here in a minute.

CHARLIE: Serves her right, to see us.

LEE: Let's go back to yours.

CHARLIE: My dad's a bit funny. What about yours?

LEE: Nah, too many kids, my sister's kids. Let's go back to yours. We can go outside.

CHARLIE: It's freezing.

Beat.

But I don't give a shit. I wanna be in the cold.

LEE: Like with Briggsy. See the bike?

CHARLIE: Yeah?

Beat.

Fuck it, yeah. My dad's got the keys, though. To the garage.

LEE: You could get them. I'd be interested to see you do it. The way you find a way. You're good at falling back on yourself, you do things, you don't just talk about them.

CHARLIE: Attitude. It runs in the family.

They exit.

Scene 8

The stage, an hour later. Darkness apart from a thin beam of light coming from a window. CHARLIE comes running on, can't find piano key, tries to get the lid off the piano. She looks distraught, has been crying. The lid won't come off the piano, so she grabs a sword from the pirates chest and tries to lever it, but it just bends. She hits piano, gives up on piano, head down on the lid. MISS FRY enters, switching on the lights.

MISS FRY: Ah, Charlie! I saw you sprinting across the back field like a…

CHARLIE: Miss.

MISS FRY: Did you hear that I'd had to take…

CHARLIE: Hello miss.

MISS FRY: Mahesh Depala sprained his bloody ankle and muggins here had a free period and ended up in casualty with him. I had to…we really needed this time, before tomorrow, but…

Beat.

CHARLIE: Tomorrow, miss?

MISS FRY: Exam?

CHARLIE: Exam. Oh yeah.

MISS FRY: Don't worry, you'll be fine – you're more than ready.

CHARLIE: Grade 1. For monkeys, that.

MISS FRY: What's going on?

Pause.

It's okay to be nervous. You get a great boost from adrenalin, it feeds the magic.

CHARLIE: The magic, yeah. Of 'There it goes at Full Gallop.' Fuck the exam. Fuck you.

MISS FRY: What?

CHARLIE: You're a fuck-up.

MISS FRY: Where has this come from?

CHARLIE: Exam? Yeah, go on, get that naughty little girl through a hoop. Looks good that.

MISS FRY: Er hang on a minute. Where has this…

CHARLIE: I christen teachers. When Glossop was crying in the corridor – her face was all ugly and black from make

up and I'm following her, I must see her face, it's too
good to miss.

MISS FRY: Okay, let's talk about this. If there's stuff at
home you…

CHARLIE: Home? Don't try and find an excuse for your…
You're a shit teacher.

MISS FRY: Right. Enough.

CHARLIE: You're fucking shameless.

MISS FRY: I said enough. I wanted to see you achieve this.
But if you can't be bothered anymore…

CHARLIE: If you re-took your teaching exams now, do
you think they would let you pass? It's like bad drivers,
innit? Lot of them about. My mum's terrible. If they
tested her again, well…can't do a three point turn and
can't handle the pedals – can't keep her legs together
long enough.

MISS FRY: Shut up, go home and calm down.

CHARLIE: You're only here cos they're desperate for
teachers.

MISS FRY: Put the sheet music to one side and…

CHARLIE: No-one listens to you.

MISS FRY: Try and remember why you're doing this.

CHARLIE: I'm doing it to please you. I respect you: Cos
you keep crawling home to get pocket money off your
parents. Do they send you out to the sweetshop when he
wants to give her one? No-one wants to know you. You're
the sad bitch who sits in dirty pubs singing about stars
and wishing someone would shove their big cock up
your arse.

MISS FRY: How dare you? Yeah, I'm a bit of a mess, so
what? And what have you got to show for yourself?

A foul mouth, a chip on your shoulder. You hate yourself so much, you'd rather end up on…

CHARLIE: You know what? I'm glad you're leaving.

MISS FRY: Charlie.

CHARLIE: I'm glad.

MISS FRY: You know.

CHARLIE: Course.

MISS FRY: I'm sorry.

CHARLIE: Don't give a shit.

CHARLIE starts to walk out.

MISS FRY: I'm leaving because of you. A vicious little kid who I thought was a write-off made me feel inspired about my own music again. You write songs on a dead piece of string. You reminded me of why I started doing this. I never stay put…another bloke, another school, another band? Then I saw a song *get* to you…for the first time…and it reminded me…I'm a musician…and I want to stick with this…no band this time. Just me and my own songs. You've got something…not in a traditional way…which is why you have to carry on, you have to do this exam tomorrow. And I don't know why I should give a shit…but if you let this thing go now, it'll be like a dropped stitch, you won't pick it up again.

CHARLIE slow handclaps her, gesturing to an audience.

CHARLIE: Pass the hat around – Quick, before they scoot off.

MISS FRY: After the exam Mr Brookes will be taking you. I've briefed everyone. Amongst all the paperwork and the rest of the crap there are some great people here.

CHARLIE: He teaches Maths.

MISS FRY: He plays and he's brilliant. He's played with a
fantastic quartet called the Blohmberg. I know you don't...

CHARLIE: The Blohmberg?

MISS FRY: Have you heard of them?

CHARLIE: Yeah. Tony Blohmberg, the band leader – he
does a turn in the Queens with Twenty Players and a
pack of pencils. Your music is boring. Alternative! It
sounds like Elton John. On a bad day, when he left his
wig in the boot of his car.

MISS FRY: Go on, pretend to be an idiot.

CHARLIE: I wanna be in the front row when you fall flat
on your face. Howling like a dog while all your mates
pretend it's good, cos you're getting too old for them to
tell you the truth.

MISS FRY: I can play.

Pause.

And I taught you to play.

She holds out a book, CHARLIE ignores it.

MISS FRY: I've written a book about you. It's for Mr
Brookes. I've detailed every single lesson we had. I tried
to remember everything from day one – at home the last
few nights with a glass of wine and a packet of fags. I'm
normally a great...adjuster, yeah, water off a duck's back,
that's my motto. But two months here and I'm flinching
every time I turn my back to the class, I'm cringing
when a fifteen-year-old boy tells me he's going to fuck
me. I'm hugging a bottle at home. But these last few
nights with the book were different. I tried to remember
everything... I was up all night...and I'd hardly touched
the wine or the...what I'm trying to say is... (*She opens
the book.*) Lesson one: how to hold your hands properly,
no Mike Tyson please. Lesson five, she whinged for half

an hour about scales and then played them perfectly. Lesson ten: she told me if I mentioned Bob Dylan again, she has an uncle who breaks legs. Silly stuff, theory and the boring basics. Most of it won't even make sense to him. Mr Brookes will know the spirit of what we've done. And more importantly who you are, what you're about. He'll customize the lessons, based on the way you've been learning. When he's not down the Kings Arms with Harry Blohmberg playing card tricks, that is. You ungrateful gobshite.

CHARLIE: The Queens, *Tony* Blohmberg. Thanks.

Pause. MISS FRY holds the book out. CHARLIE takes it.

CHARLIE: I have learned something, miss. I've understood what you said once about music making you vanish. Into thin air: (*Starting to rip up the book.*) Teaching – a month here, a month there and a puff of smoke! This band, that band and a puff of smoke! You were the kid who was crap at staring people out. Looked away as soon as your eyes watered.

MISS FRY: This place is hard work.

CHARLIE: I've managed.

MISS FRY: You're not a teacher. Stuck in the middle of nowhere, with a bunch of thick as shit kids.

CHARLIE: Thick as shit teachers.

MISS FRY: Go on, act like one of your brain-dead friends.

CHARLIE: That's what you didn't get in the book. What I'm really about. You don't remember how it is when your mates *get* the same things you do. You see it, you clock it, you crack up. It's not even funny, but these guys are with you all the way. Course, that's not the only attraction – you didn't get the pages of me *in my element.*

MISS FRY: Yeah, it's so funny being the town slag.

CHARLIE: Yeah, I love it.

MISS FRY: The leg spreader, there she goes.

CHARLIE: That's what she's best at. Half hour ago she had Lee Coulson outside her garage. He made me come so hard.

MISS FRY: Go on – piss the rest of your life up the wall. Until it's written all over your face, what you are. That woman in McDonalds with the dead eyes. Forty something and still finding her name on toilet walls... You think that won't be you? And what a laugh – Queuing up for your dole cheque, daytime telly, drunk by the middle of the day. Why not you? And you won't have any mates – they'll all be inside or they'll have had you so many times they'll be sick of the smell of you. I got out of here, I know...

CHARLIE: You're back we're you started.

MISS FRY: Wrong. I've got choices now.

CHARLIE: After we'd done it, I showed him my bike. And it was like the icing on the cake. They all want to see my bike. I unlock the padlock, we're in the garage and the broom goes flying, but we don't notice, we're just gazing at the bike in the half light. Drinking it in.

MISS FRY: You know this is crap, Charlie.

CHARLIE: The frost is cracking the window panes and both our breath is in the air. And he flicks on the torch and lights up that bike.

MISS FRY: You're not a coward. I saw you give yourself up to a song. You were terrified.

CHARLIE: He saw every single inch of my bike – leaning on its stand and casting a shadow. Black and chrome that shines like silver. His mouth fell open, he...

MISS FRY: I won't let you be a bully, a loser.

CHARLIE: It was worth the wait, he said, it's….

MISS FRY: I won't let you throw your life away.

CHARLIE: …it's a dream, He said it's…

MISS FRY: Like your brother did.

Silence.

CHARLIE: When we got to the garage…I tried to…kiss him but he wanted to see the bike.

Pause.

…It took me ages to undo the padlock…cos my hands were shaking so much…and this is me, I take people on. Then a can went crunch under his feet and the broom went flying and I goes 'the noise!' But he was sort of gawping…at the bike, he didn't hear… But it was half in…we couldn't see…needed a light. I said… 'there's no torch, let's go.' But his foot kicked against one and he said 'it's here' and he flicked on the switch. There was a glare, it moved around the garage, it found the bike… and he ran a spotlight over the Hollister. Then he started to…he was listing things, making them up. Look at the rust, look at the paintwork, it's on its way out. It's full of holes, it's washed up. It won't go, it won't start. It's dirty, it's pock marked. It still goes, I said. It's a beauty, this bike of mine. It's black, it's chrome. It's the light that's wrong. Because it's my bike.

MISS FRY: It's not your bike.

CHARLIE: It's mine.

MISS FRY: It's not your bike.

CHARLIE: But he didn't listen.

MISS FRY: It wasn't the truth.

CHARLIE: I told him.

MISS FRY: Who's bike is it?

CHARLIE: Mine.

MISS FRY: Who's bike is it?

CHARLIE: I'm alone.

MISS FRY: You're not.

CHARLIE: I'm alone.

MISS FRY: You're not.

CHARLIE: He was the Hollister Boy, he was always at the front.

MISS FRY hesitates, then goes to hold her. She holds her for a long time.

CHARLIE: This is me, I take people on.

MISS FRY: This is me, water off a duck's back.

Long pause.

You're not…

Beat.

CHARLIE: What?

MISS FRY: …the bike girl.

Pause.

CHARLIE: I'm not the piano one.

MISS FRY: I think…

Beat.

It's just my opinion.

Beat.

I think you are.

Pause.

It must be…so hard sometimes.

CHARLIE: It's alright for you.

MISS FRY: Yes, I say I understand, but obviously…

CHARLIE: No, I mean… You're the one who drops things and don't iron her clothes. That's the one you are. So you're okay.

MISS FRY: I'm her tomorrow and someone else the next day.

CHARLIE: I dunno miss, I think you've been quite consistent with it.

MISS FRY: You see me in a classroom.

CHARLIE: I know.

Silence.

MISS FRY: Why don't you play me something?

CHARLIE: No, you're alright.

MISS FRY: You're going to play. Or I'm going to play. No arguments. Let's find this piano key.

MISS FRY is rummaging through her bag.

MISS FRY: There's a hole in this bloody bag. I can't see anything in here. I'll find it in a minute, we really should do this… Fuck it.

MISS FRY puts the bag down and puts her head in her hands. Pause.

CHARLIE: I'll find it.

CHARLIE grabs MISS FRY's bag, rummages around and can't find anything. Eventually she tips it all out onto the floor.

CHARLIE: Don't worry. Urgh, what's that? Miss?

MISS FRY: A sandwich, sorry, try the pocket.

CHARLIE: Oh miss, it's like my dad's shoes in here, you've gotta sort it out.

MISS FRY: There it is.

CHARLIE: No, it's a 50p.

MISS FRY: Is it?

CHARLIE: And it's got a grape on it.

MISS FRY: Put it down.

CHARLIE: Urgh, it's not a grape, what is it?

MISS FRY: Look, there it is.

CHARLIE: What is it?

MISS FRY: The key is there, there.

CHARLIE: But if it's not a grape…?

MISS FRY: Charlie, please.

CHARLIE hands the key to her.

You play.

CHARLIE: (*Putting the key on top of the piano.*) In a bit.

Pause.

MISS FRY: I think I'll just step out and…

CHARLIE: It's cold out, miss.

MISS FRY: I know it's…

CHARLIE: Freezing, it's…

MISS FRY: I never seem to notice it.

CHARLIE: Neither do I.

MISS FRY: (*Grabbing her cigarettes.*) Fresh air, then.

Pause.

If I'm not back in ten… I've copped off with the caretaker.

MISS FRY exits. CHARLIE looks lost for a moment. She snaps out of it, goes to unlock the piano.

She starts to play a tune and uses her 'day' system to pick out the notes and sing very quietly along to it.

CHARLIE: Thursday--Saturday afternoon----Friday--Wednesday afternoon----Friday--Thursday----Friday--noneday----

Thursday--Saturday afternoon----Friday--Wednesday afternoon----Friday--Thursday----Friday--noneday----

The End.